People and Chips

The Human Implications of Information Technology

People and Chips

The Human Implications of Information Technology

Christopher Rowe

Paradigm Publishing

Paradigm Publishing
140 Kensington Church Street
London W8 4BN

First edition 1986

© C. Rowe 1986

British Library Cataloguing in Publication Data

Rowe, Christopher
  People and Chips: the human implications
  of information technology.
  1. Technological innovations—Social
  aspects
  I. Title
  303.4′83   T173.8

  ISBN 0–948825–00–6

Typeset by Mathematical Composition Setters Ltd, Salisbury and
Printed in Great Britain by Hollen Street Press Ltd, Slough, Berks.

Preface

On Friday, 31 March 1978, the BBC showed a *Horizon* programme called 'Now the chips are down' which is generally acknowledged as the moment when Britain first became aware of the 'microchip'. Since then we have been inundated with paperbacks, TV programmes, government reports, and a host of other pontifications as to whether — to quote the marriage service — this will be for better or worse, for richer or poorer, or even whether it will lead to sickness or health. We are told that every aspect of life will be affected, and so vast and varied have been the outpourings that it has seemed impossible at times — particularly as regards the human effects — to disentangle and make sense of them. This book attempts to rectify that situation.

My own interest in new technology emerged through preparing and teaching undergraduate courses, and through work in industry. The ideas for this book had been germinating in my mind for some time, but it stems directly from the 1984 London Computing Conference when Alfred Waller was kind enough to invite me to prepare a book on the human implications of new information technology.

It is impossible to mention all those who have either directly or indirectly helped to formulate my ideas, but I am most grateful to students, colleagues and industrial contacts, and to David Brown, Anthony Norris, Tony Thomas and Adrian Walker, who read the entire manuscript at various stages. Howard Davies was a great help with Chapter 3, as was Liz Bird with Chapter 7, and Jerry Booth with Chapter 8.

Acknowledgements are also gratefully given to all authors whose work is quoted, and to their publishers for granting permission to reproduce this material.

ACKNOWLEDGMENTS

The author and publisher are grateful to those cited, for permission to reproduce the following material:

Extract from *Trends in Information Technology: 1985*, published by Arthur Andersen & Co., Chicago.

Extract from Cooley, M. (1984) Computers, Politics and Unemployment, in Sieghart (ed.) *Microchips with Everything*, published by Comedia, London.

Extracts from Jenkins, C. & Sherman, B. (1979) *The Collapse of Work*, published by Methuen, London.

Extract from Masuda, Y. (1981) The information society as post-industrial society. Reprinted from THE FUTURIST, published by the World Future Society, 4916 St. Elmo Ave., Bethesda, MD 20814.

Figure from Parker, S. (1983) *Leisure and Work*, reproduced by permission of George Allen & Unwin, London.

Figure from Rowan, T. (1982) *Managing with Computers*, reproduced by permission of Pan Books, London.

Extracts from Taylor, F. W. (1911) *The Principles of Scientific Management*, published by Harper & Row, New York.

Figure from Watson, T. J. (1980) *Sociology, Work and Industry*, reproduced by permission of the publishers, Routledge & Kegan Paul, London.

Illustration from Zorkoczy, P. (1985) *Information Technology: An Introduction* (2nd edn), reprinted by permission of Pitman Publishing Ltd, London.

Contents

CHAPTER ONE

Introduction

It is a sobering thought that by the time you read this book much of the technology it discusses will have radically altered. This is not to suggest you should stop reading — on the contrary, a major theme is that the issues raised are irresolvable and on-going and will be as alive at the turn of the century as they are today — but merely to acknowledge the astonishing pace of technological change.

Most of this change stems from that burgeoning branch of science known as microelectronics, and in particular the development of a device no bigger than a thumbnail, no thicker than a leaf, which is popularly known as the 'silicon chip'. Millions of chips are already in use. In the home they are found in cookers and refrigerators, telephones and cars, watches and TV games; in the factory they control assembly lines, machine tools and paint sprays; in offices they are contained in word processors and photocopy machines; in supermarkets, banks and garages they are found in cash registers, automatic teller machines and petrol pumps. Hotel and theatre bookings, banking, news-gathering, weather forecasting, medical analysis, you name it — all are being transformed by new technology.

However, this is not a book about the technology itself — how it works and what it does — so much as a discussion of the possible effects it could have upon people. Some predict it will usher in a totally new and better form of society, while others fear it will exacerbate many of the less desirable features of present-day living. This book considers that debate and draws on sociology, economics, law and politics to explore the central question of the human effects of new technology.

Consequently I shall not say a great deal on definitions and terminology. I shall refer to microelectronics to identify that wide field of technological development that incorporates and applies electronic components or circuits made to very small dimensions, but recognize that it is when the chip is linked with other new developments — particularly in computing and telecommunications — that its true significance becomes apparent. It is this convergence — relating to the creation, transmission, manipulation and presentation of data — that has spawned such labels as 'new information technology', 'micro-technology', or simply 'new technology'. None of these can be precisely defined because the pace of change and range of applications is such that this is not possible. I may well use the labels interchangeably and trust I shall be forgiven for not spending time distinguishing between them.

My task is to consider ways in which life in the future, whether at work or in the home, will be affected. There are no simple answers to this, and in exploring the human effects I am less concerned with providing solutions than raising issues. A major theme is that what we expect to result from technology is largely determined by the way we look at it. Therefore, I do not suggest what *will* happen, but rather consider what *might* or could happen. My aim is not to preach a particular 'line' but to examine the various lines already being preached. I shall particularly focus upon work, partly because this is where much of the debate has centred, but also because it is here that my special interests lie. In a short book such as this, I cannot hope to cover every human aspect, and work is given special prominence. I shall also largely restrict myself to a discussion of Britain.

NEW INFORMATION TECHNOLOGY

Why should so many claim that the microchip is revolutionary and will transform human society as we know it? After all, the functions it performs are essentially no different to those of earlier computers, and all that has happened is that scientists have been able to pack increasing numbers of components on to small pieces of silicon. The chip's distinctiveness, and why many regard it as a 'breakthrough technology', can be summarized under five simple headings.

Size

The continuing trend towards miniaturization has made it possible to now contain a million components on a chip of silicon 1 centimetre square. This is known as very large-scale integration (VLSI), and with further developments in photographic techniques it is thought that over a hundred million components could be contained on one chip. Chips can now be mounted on an A4 board to provide a microcomputer equivalent to a whole office of equipment of just fifteen years ago. This allows small, light computing power to be installed in an increasing range of products and applications, and offers enormous gains in terms of space. A complete microprocessor computer — the INMOS transputer — can even be put on to one chip, and the next step will be to construct cooperative arrays of such computers so that they can work in parallel on enormously complex problems.

Cost

Despite the continual rise in the cost of almost everything else over the past twenty years, the prices of electronic components have actually *fallen* at an increasing rate. In 1956 a transistor cost around three pounds: this was halved a year later and today costs no more than a few pence. The same applies to integrated circuits, which cost around twenty pounds in 1960 but were nearer twenty pence by 1970. Silicon is one of the world's most available resources and, almost yearly, costs have continued to tumble at around 30 per cent while the complexity of integrated circuits has doubled. The substitution of microelectronic components in various products reduces their cost, not only because the devices themselves are cheap to make, but also because they make possible massive savings in energy consumption, maintenance, testing, floor-space and back-up facilities.

Reliability

The microchip is thousands of times more reliable than the electronic components of the 1950s, and this has dramatically affected the manufacture of many products, e.g. calculators and watches. Digital watches costing forty pounds in the mid-1970s were down to five pounds by the 1980s, and captured 50 per cent of the market in ten years because of their greater reliability and flexibility. Similarly in the field of robotics, increased reliability means that microprocessor-controlled robots can now work in environments hostile to human beings, such as sewers, coal mines, paint spray shops and oil rigs.

Capacity
Thanks to the chip, the memory capacity and processing power of microcomputers has increased so rapidly that they now offer similar capacity to earlier mainframe computers. During the 1970s, microchips increased their capacity 10 000 times over, and this has allowed microelectronics to become a 'heartland' technology. It now affects *all* sectors of industry and commerce, for chips can be used in robots, data banks, telephone exchanges and many other operations.

Speed
The chip means that microcomputers today are over forty times as fast as the famous ENIAC machine of 1946, and there is every sign that processing speeds will continue to rise. A microcomputer today can 'read' the Bible in less than 5 seconds and retain every word of it. Development work is now being done on a gallium arsenide chip, five times faster than its silicon rival, which can do calculations in 80 picoseconds; 1 picosecond being 1 million-millionth of a second.

To summarize, a good microcomputer today is forty times as fast, has a memory 400 times as great, is 1500 times smaller, costs one ten-thousandth as much, is 17 000 times lighter, uses 2800 times less power, and is thousands of times more reliable, than ENIAC, the first electronic computer. Or to take an oft-quoted comparative example: if the motor industry had developed at the same speed as the computer industry, then a Rolls-Royce today would cost around three pounds, it would do 3 million miles to the gallon, its speed would be staggering, and one could put five on a fingertip. Similarly, if the aerospace industry had developed at the same pace, a Boeing 767 would cost just 400 pounds and could circle the earth on only five gallons of fuel, while Concorde would have been flying nine months after the Wright brothers took off.

Forms of application
The range of applications is of course enormous, but they can be conveniently grouped within four general categories:

- They can serve as the basis for new products, e.g. digital watches, calculators, word processors etc.
- They can replace conventional circuitry in existing products, e.g. car components, TV components etc.
- They can change the production process itself, e.g. robotics.
- They can affect basic information systems, e.g. System X in telecommunications.

Over the past few years we have become increasingly familiar with the first two applications, but it is in relation to the latter two that the greater long-term effects can be expected. Particularly in Britain, the impact of robotics and information technology has been modest to date, but dramatic changes could well occur before the turn of the century. In *The Mighty Micro*, Christopher Evans (1979) divided this period into three sections: the short-term future (1980–2), the middle-term future (1983–90) and the long-term future (1990–2000). He predicted that in the short term we would simply become aware of micro technology — start to play computer games, wear digital wristwatches and replace our pencils with calculators — which is very much what happened. But after this a rapid acceleration of change could be expected. Just as we have difficulty conceiving the scale of such current problems as global food shortages, energy crises or atmospheric pollution, so, Evans argues, we remain largely oblivious to what could occur.

Already chips are allowing scientists to devise machines that can 'talk' to the deaf, that translate written sentences from one language to another, and that replace workers on assembly lines. Robots can now walk on other planets and dig up samples; the Japanese have devised machines that can play Bach on an organ and draw portraits in two minutes; and people will soon be watching TV on their wristwatches. The field of artificial intelligence allows us to create machines with 'knowledge' that can increasingly supplant man's brain power as well as his muscle power. No area of human activity seems likely to remain unaffected, particularly as the various forms of new technology increasingly converge.

In considering the pervasiveness of micro-technology, one can perhaps draw useful parallels from the first industrial revolution. The steam engine — generally considered one of the key inventions — was initially used solely for pumping water out of mines, and this it did most effectively for half a century. Only when it was

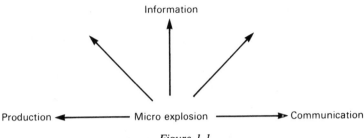

Figure 1.1

linked with other technologies, however, did it become a true heartland technology: fitted to a wagon it created a locomotive; added to a loom it provided a power loom. Similarly today, it is when the microchip is linked to other (mainly twentieth-century) technologies that its significance becomes fully apparent: when linked with a typewriter and television screen we obtain a word processor; when added to a machine we create a robot.

It is the elements of pervasiveness and technological convergence that I wish to stress, and to consider in relation to social and industrial life. In the short term it is in the field of *information* that the most immediate effects are being felt (with the introduction of microcomputers, word processors etc.), but equally important will be developments with regard to *production* (e.g. robotics, computer-aided design (CAD), computer-aided manufacture (CAM), lasers etc.) and *communication* (e.g. cable systems, satellites, telecommunications etc.). This can be represented as a 'micro explosion' affecting all areas of human existence (*see* Fig. 1.1).

While we have experienced change before, Evans believes that the social repercussions from the chip will be of such magnitude as to totally alter our society and present way of living. Social institutions, work patterns, beliefs and attitudes, political structures — all will be transformed out of recognition.

TECHNOLOGY AND SOCIETY

There is no doubt that technology can greatly affect society: we only have to think of the impact of the motor car or television on our own age to see this. But the danger with Evans's approach, and those who similarly laud the potential of new information technology, is that they rather present the technology as though it operates in a vacuum, apart from political and economic forces. The relationship is not mono-causal; for just as technology affects society so, in its turn, society influences technology, both in terms of its research and development, and in relation to its application and control. We need to pause for a moment to consider this.

When we think of technological breakthroughs we tend to envisage the process starting with a research idea — 'the eureka moment' — which then leads to applications and products. At this point — when the technology is applied to the market — inventions become innovations, and diffusion occurs as new technologies replace old (e.g. transistors replacing valves). This, however, rather suggests that technological development is an 'independent variable', operating in isolation from social forces, and transforming society the moment it becomes available. In reality, this is not the case, for technology is also a 'social product', largely determined by those who hold and administer power at a given time. Technology now becomes the 'dependent variable', and innovation more significant than invention. One can illustrate this with reference to the great 'inventions' of the first industrial revolution. In a sense they were not inventions at all, but rather applications — innovations when the economic situation was ripe — by practical business men. The theoretical, scientific knowledge on which many machines were based had been available for over a century, and there are countless examples where societies do not innovate technologically even though the knowledge exists. Braverman (1974), for instance, notes how artificial dyes based on coal tar were developed in Germany but not Britain because the latter could import dyes from the colonies. It is true that the distinction has become increasingly blurred as large companies now employ research and development staff to both invent *and* innovate, but it is analytically useful for our purposes.

The distinction is important in the work of Nikolai Kondratiev (1925), the Russian economist who argued that economic development always proceeds in waves, and the key to technological innovation is not some inspired moment of invention so much as the current level of economic activity; innovations being more likely in periods of economic recession. According to his theory, the Western world was due for a down-turn during the 1970s —

precisely what happened — and we are unlikely to return to substantial growth before the end of the 1990s. He would maintain we are presently in the fourth 'wave' — experiencing considerable technological innovation at a time of economic recession — and will not move into a fifth until the mid-1990s. It is the entrepreneurs (the innovators) rather than the scientists (the inventors) who therefore provide the fuse for new technological applications, investment, growth and employment.

This suggests that it might be dangerous to imply that a particular technology *causes* a certain type of society; for while it is true that any technology contains societal implications, its actual introduction, and therefore the resulting socio-economic effects, also to a considerable extent reflect the nature of that society. Technology does not just 'happen' but is largely dependent on governmental and corporate action in making funds available for scientific research. It is therefore very much a social product.

For example, the reason we have experienced silicon chips over the past decade is not simply because someone chanced to discover that silicon could be used as a semi-conductive material, but also that the United States government, desperate to maintain its defences and stay in the space race with the Soviet Union, invested enormous sums towards providing smaller, lighter computers for spacecraft and weapon systems. Had the same research effort gone in other directions, we might today have a cure for cancer, or whatever.

TECHNOLOGY AND CHOICE

A new technology is therefore to a considerable extent a social product but, more than this, once it comes into existence, its actual application can proceed in very different directions. For example, electricity may be used to provide people with light and heating or to execute them; the American space programme not only placed a man on the moon but gave us non-stick frying pans and improved hearing aids; and at the present time, lasers are being developed which can be deployed in 'star wars' defence programmes or applied to medical surgery (such as the removal of brain tumours) or the coding of manufactured products.

Technology, as regards its application, is therefore also a matter for human choice. One cannot say technology is 'good' or 'bad', 'appropriate' or 'inappropriate'; this all depends on what we as human beings choose to do with it. The extent to which technology determines society, or how much it is a social product, and whether we as individuals can affect the outcome, therefore provides a 'three-cornered' arena for debate. The danger with Evans is that he rather implies that particular developments will *automatically* happen, while others fear the uses of technology will be totally controlled by those holding economic and political power. Both views rather play down the element of choice, which I shall suggest is important, for the more we as people are aware of the alternatives, the more effectively — both collectively and individually — we can influence the outcome. The aim of this book is to increase that awareness.

In the work sphere, for instance, there is no doubt that manufacturing and commerce can be increasingly mechanized and automated by microelectronic devices, but this is no more than a technological capability which could be realized in many different ways. Work can be reskilled or deskilled, expanded or destroyed. What is technologically *possible* should not be confused with what is *probable*, for the actual human and social consequences of new technology remain uncertain. We may know what technology can do, but how it will be applied remains contentious; a matter for debate, a matter of choice.

Finally, even when we focus upon a particular application, we cannot make objective judgements as to the effects of the technology. For instance, has the motor car been a benefit to society? Clearly, on one side, it has greatly assisted transport and communication and enabled people to visit parts of the world that would otherwise have remained inaccessible to them; but, on the other hand, it has resulted in traffic jams on overcrowded motorways, new forms of crime, polluted air and serious accidents. Despite increased technological sophistication, the average car now travels through London at a slower speed than at the start of the century. Progress? Many now question this. Technology seems to raise as many problems as it solves, and those who preach the 'new millennium' are increasingly viewed with suspicion. More now see technology as a 'mixed blessing', conceding that there are both plusses and minuses. How one sees this 'mix' is therefore a highly personal, subjective matter. To take the most obvious (and fearful) example of modern technology, nuclear weaponry: whether one views this as a danger or a benefit depends on one's own particular standpoint. It's a technology no one actually wants to use, but if you see nuclear weapons as a threat to the survival of our entire planet, then you see them as a 'bad thing', whereas if you consider they provide a deterrent to political adversaries who threaten a form of society you hold dear, and make war less likely because they provide a 'power-balance' between the super-powers, then you see them as necessary, justified and beneficial.

There is no uniform approach to new technology. Our response is increasingly uncertain: hopes and expectations mixed with doubts and misgivings. It creates responsibilities and moral dilemmas which we feel ill-equipped to handle even though we possess greater knowledge and control over nature than ever before. It is as though we have created an awesome monster we feel unable to contain. Thanks to technology, we can live longer (and more healthily) in a fuller, richer life, but we can also burn up in a few decades the oil created over millions of years. We can expand our travel and leisure facilities but at the same time pollute rivers, destroy rain forests and gravely endanger rare animal species. We can provide the world with sophisticated drugs and chemicals yet suffer the kind of human disaster that occurred at the Union Carbide chemical plant in Bhopal, India, in 1984, when 2500 were killed and thousands injured following a gas leak at the factory. Is technology a boon? In particular, how do these issues relate to the chip?

The central concern of this book is therefore with the interface between society and technology — especially new information technology — and the choices we as people can make. Clearly the matter is subjective and highly contentious. It shows why there is an irreconcilable debate as to whether technologies such as microelectronics represent a 'revolution' or merely a further 'evolutionary' stage in technological and social development: something radically new or simply 'more of the same'. Will it create a fresh form of society, or does it rather provide further tools for those who presently hold economic and political power to entrench their position? Moreover, is technology (in whatever form) something we simply have to accept, or can we — as humans and citizens — exercise choice in the matter? If so, how much and in what form? And, most important, if this is inadequate, what do we propose to do about it?

Clearly we shall experience significant change, but what is far less certain is the precise form and direction it will take, the rate at which it will occur, and the effects it will have. These issues are debatable; and we cannot say one view is right and another wrong, for they represent different *perspectives* — different ways of looking at technology and society. Technology — like beauty — is clearly very much in the eye of the beholder; a subjective rather than an objective matter. To paraphrase Marx: what we see does not determine our perspective; on the contrary, it is our perspective that determines what we see. This explains the diversity of views from those who prophesy a 'Utopian tomorrow' to those who warn of 'Orwellian totalitarianism'. The key question of perspectives is considered further in the next chapter and provides a framework for the remainder of the book.

CHAPTER TWO

Contrasting Perspectives

A common theme since 1978 — when people in Britain first began to talk about microelectronics — is that 'western society is experiencing a series of technological revolutions which is changing our society and our economy as profoundly as did the Industrial Revolution' (Stonier, 1979). Just as people's working lives were transformed by the invention of the spinning jenny, the steam engine, electric generation and the internal combustion engine, so it is argued that the microchip will have an equivalent impact. Writing in 1978, Tom Forester suggested that 'the invention of the chip represents a quantum leap in technology far more important than the clumsy great computers of the 1950s, and it could be as important as the discovery of electricity itself'. Other writers have similarly maintained that the industrialized world is on the brink of economic and structural upheaval and that the microchip will create a new society which has variously been described as post-industrial society (Bell, 1974, 1979), the third wave (Toffler, 1980) and the information society (Masuda, 1981).

Many find such predictions premature and overblown. One view — which I reject — argues that the chip is simply a further stage in technological advancement and that society will adjust as it always has in the past. I would label this the 'complacency view' for it totally underestimates the chip's potential and the degree of change we might expect. A more subtle response is one that acknowledges the chip as an astonishing device and accepts that change will occur, but questions whether this necessarily means wholescale social transformation. Are we justified in talking of a micro *revolution*, or any other kind of revolution? We need to consider the word revolution carefully for it can be applied in various forms — technological, industrial, social, political — and though these are invariably intertwined we may experience one apart from the others, or one form may clearly precede another. The fact that the chip is small, cheap and highly reliable could mean that it is revolutionary in a technological sense — but no more than this — and it might perhaps be better seen as merely a further (if important) stage of scientific advancement.

THE FIRST INDUSTRIAL REVOLUTION

The industrial revolution is the term used to describe the changes that occurred — first in Britain between 1780 and 1830 and then in other parts of the world — to mark the transition from agricultural production to manufacturing. Britain changed from an agricultural country, with a small population, a low standard of living, a hierarchical social structure and a ruling aristocratic oligarchy, to a nation dependent on manufacturing and extractive industries, with a large population, growing urban centres, increasing social mobility, greater political democracy and vastly increased wealth. Virtually no English institution or aspect of life remained untouched by these changes; and not only was more produced, but work was done in new ways.

When writing of the first industrial revolution, Phyllis Deane (1965) identifies a series of fundamental changes which she suggests characterized the period. She argues that these inter-related changes, if they develop together and to a sufficient degree, constitute an industrial revolution. It is not just changing technology that is important, but the fact that it brings forth fresh ways of living. Deane lists seven main features that characterize an industrial revolution.

● Widespread and systematic application of science and knowledge to the process of production for the market

The first industrial revolution was dramatically affected by certain key inventions, which allowed for massive increases in output and created spin-off effects throughout the rest of the economy.

● Specialization of economic activity for wide markets

Manufacturers began to mass-produce goods for the market which could then be sold at a profit to provide for further capital investment.

● Movement of population

In 1780, England's population was 9.7 million and nearly 80 per cent lived and worked in the countryside. By 1830 there were fourteen English towns over 50 000 and Britain became rapidly urbanized.

● The movement of labour between employment sectors.

Agricultural employment fell from 75 per cent of the total labour force in 1688 to 50 per cent by 1780, 25 per cent by 1840, and 3 per cent by 1980, even though production increased nearly seventy-fold thanks to new technology. The agricultural revolution thereby stimulated the industrial revolution, which in turn stimulated a service revolution, fresh labour being released in each instance.

● The growth of new units of production and patterns of work

Small-scale, domestic production was replaced by large-scale, factory production. A switch occurred from 'natural power' (water, animals, wind etc.) to inanimate, calculable power, based first on steam and later on electricity and atomic energy. Changing work patterns also demanded a disciplined, time-conscious work force. Workers had to develop new attitudes to time, morals, drink, thrift etc., as work became governed by the clock rather than the sun and the seasons.

● Intensive and extensive use of capital resources

Capital became a substitute for, and complement to, human effort. This stimulated the development of technology, which resulted in intensified mechanization, automation and the sub-division of workers' tasks.

● The emergence of new social and occupational classes

Industrial capitalism was a fresh mode of production which threw up new social classes: the bourgeoisie and proletariat. The former's power rested on its ownership of capital in the form of property, machinery, raw materials etc. Labour power became bought and sold as a commodity, and profit determined work relations and the development and utilization of technology.

The first industrial revolution therefore involved not only significant technological change but also dramatic *social* transformation. In the light of present-day developments, are we justified in talking of a 'new industrial revolution' and can we expect changes of similar magnitude? In particular, can we expect these changes to occur as a direct result of the application of new forms of technology?

A NEW INDUSTRIAL REVOLUTION?

One writer who believes we are now experiencing change on a similar scale to that of the first industrial revolution is Daniel Bell, who argues that just as we moved from pre-industrial to industrial society so now we are moving into a new form of society that is best termed 'post-industrial'. He argues that knowledge (and especially scientific knowledge) is acquiring a centrality in society that it previously did not have and that authority (based on knowledge) is now more important than ownership of property. 'Technocrats' are the dominant elite rather than the bourgeoisie, and developments in microelectronics and 'intellectual technology' are encouraging this process. The imperatives of technology, not the forces of ideology, now determine the shape of society.

If we revert to Deane's seven characteristics, Bell would argue that they apply as much today as they did two centuries ago.

- Widespread and systematic application of science and knowledge to the process of production for the market

Scientific knowledge and its application now become *more* important as decisions are increasingly taken by technocrats who base their judgements on scientific expertise rather than entrepreneurial flair. More decisions can be programmed as computers are used for decision-making, and forecasts made by universities, research units, professionals etc. increasingly override the views of politicians, businessmen and others. Knowledge becomes the guide to action.

- Specialization of economic activity for wide markets

Economic activity encourages even greater specialization as new products are developed and sold in ever-widening markets. The activity takes on a new form in that instead of imperial powers exploiting their colonies for raw materials and markets, trade now occurs within large economic units (e.g. the European Economic Community) and products are manufactured and sold by multi-national companies the world over.

● Movement of population

While people previously moved from the countryside into the towns, they now switch from the inner-city areas to the suburbs, as new work patterns emerge. People also move between regions, and just as the north of England experienced population growth during the first industrial revolution, so now future expansion will occur in the south.

● The movement of labour between employment sectors

As people moved from the primary to the secondary manufacturing sector, so now increasingly they transfer to the service or tertiary sector. Bell even argues that with two-thirds now in service employment, this sector can itself be usefully sub-divided — between those who provide services based on the transfer of information and those who do not. Stonier predicts that by the turn of the century 40 per cent could work in what he terms 'the knowledge industry', and Jones (1982) suggests that this will represent a further 'post-service' stage (*see* Fig. 2.1).

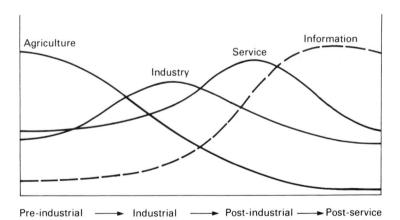

Figure 2.1   Towards a post-service society

● The growth of new units of production and patterns of work

Mundane factory and office tasks will be taken over by technology, and workers freed from the constraints of industrial work patterns. No longer will they need to assemble together at the same time and place, and more will work from home. The new technologies will provide our basic needs and allow greater time for education, travel, sport and other leisure activities.

● Intensive and extensive use of capital resources

Capital investment again plays a crucial role in stimulating new technological development, but now it takes a different form. Whereas in the eighteenth century, investment came principally from entrepreneurial businessmen — 'talented tinkerers', as Bell terms them — investment in the post-industrial economy comes overwhelmingly from national governments, multi-national corporations and large-scale research organizations. This is due to the considerable cost and complexity of modern technological research.

● The emergence of new social and occupational classes

Finally, as work organizations grow in size and complexity, so control becomes concentrated in the hands of the technocrats and specialist managers, while ownership is diluted due to the growth of joint stock companies. The managers are more 'socially responsible' than the exploiting bourgeoisie, developing a 'corporate conscience' and remaining neutral between capital and labour. The growth of managers, professionals and white-collar workers makes obsolete the Marxist view of society polarized between bourgeoisie and proletariat. This is replaced by a more open, fluid, meritocratic and pluralist society. Expertise becomes dispersed, with experts in one functional area providing checks and balances on those in another.

Bell suggests we are experiencing a new industrial revolution in that Deane's seven characteristics apply as much today as they did in the eighteenth century. Microelectronics represents such a leap in technological advancement, and its influence will be so widespread, that we should prepare to leave the industrial age for post-industrial society. This view is shared by Alvin Toffler who believes that human experience has gone through 'three waves' — agricultural, industrial and post-industrial — and that while the first covered thousands of years, and the second 300, the third (which began around 1955) will 'sweep across history and complete itself in a few decades'. Thus we are at the clashing of the waves, with the third hitting the second before, in many parts of the world, the first has even spent its force. Similarly, Masuda talks of 'Computopia' — a new information-based society.

All these writers tend to see technological development as a virtually autonomous force which compels society to adapt to it — what critics would call 'technological determinism'. According to this model, societies are classified by the stage of technological development they have reached, and we in effect do this when we refer to the stone age, bronze age, steam age, nuclear age, computer age, and so on. A dominant technology is taken as the overriding influence on a given historical epoch. Moreover, as society is determined by the nature of its technology, it is assumed that societies at parallel stages of technological development will be similar in other respects, and this should encourage greater harmony between them.

AN OPTIMISTIC VIEWPOINT

These writers adopt a highly *optimistic* standpoint, for they view technological change as 'progressive' — leading to a 'better' society in terms of material benefits, work satisfaction, enhanced freedoms, greater consensus, more leisure time etc. Nowhere is this more apparent than in the work of Kerr *et al.* (1973, 1983) who argue that convergence is occurring not just in the technological realm, but in a broader, social sense. The essence of their 'convergence thesis' is that industrialism — and the technological advances it implies — has brought with it certain inevitable changes in social life and imposed common patterns of social behaviour, i.e. societies that have industrialized have 'converged' and become increasingly alike. Put simply, the suggestion is that whether one is in London, Los Angeles or Moscow, cities now look increasingly alike with skyscraper blocks, supermarkets, cars, television etc., and this is primarily the result of universal technology. Microelectronics will only intensify this. The 'internal logic of industrialism' has been disseminated from Britain to Europe, the United States, Russia and Japan by the pressures of world-wide military technology and trade, and this will eventually embrace the whole world. Certain key characteristics are now found in all industrialized countries, including large-scale mechanized factory production; high levels of technical skill and professional competence; considerable social, occupational and geographical mobility; universal education that stresses science and technology; 'large-scale society' based on mass production, large cities, big government, large bureaucracies etc.; a reduction of national cultural differences and an impetus towards consensus on values; a central role for government in the development of transport, welfare and broadcasting; and the universal development of industrialism which should lead to a reduction in world conflict. Thus a distinctive consensus develops, within free, pluralist societies which relates individuals and groups to each other and provides an integrated framework of ideas, ideologies and values. Fresh technological advances such as microelectronics further these developments, and allow post-industrial society to become a world-wide phenomenon.

Modern telecommunications illustrate the point. Whereas the British government did not know of the American declaration of independence in 1776 until a sailing ship had crossed the Atlantic to tell them, the Live Aid TV concerts in 1985 were able to reach a world-wide audience of 1.5 billion in 169 countries and make us universally aware of the African famine. Similarly in Germany, we can see how, despite political and military attempts to create two separate societies in the east and west, satellites now make it possible for citizens of each state to see the other's television programmes. Technology thus provides a convergence that supersedes political frontiers; what has been termed a 'global village'.

There may still be differences between societies but these are now less important, Kerr argues, than the things that bind them together. Similarly, there may still be social differences *within* societies, but these will increasingly fade with growing affluence, and as conflict becomes contained within agreed rules and norms. The two overriding implications of the convergence thesis are that we can expect less divisiveness thanks to new technology, and therefore 'third world' countries should be encouraged and assisted to follow the same path, through industrialization, to post-industrial society.

Put simply, all these writers depict a utopian tomorrow. They *like* the new technology; marvel at its potential; welcome its introduction; and are confident of the social benefits. So vast will be the change that they think it realistic to speak of a new industrial revolution and to expect a fresh social order. The chip will free mankind from the toils of labour and domestic chores; release it from the fears of war and crime; allow superior services in health and education; permit greater democratic participation; and generally provide a higher quality of life. The technology is presented as liberating and positive. In that such writers are generally uncritical of existing society, and highly supportive of the material benefits that could accrue from technological advancement, their viewpoint gains considerable support from the political right.

THE PESSIMISTIC VIEWPOINT

In contrast, there are many who are far less exuberant about the coming of new technology. This distinction — between 'optimists' and 'pessimists' — has already been touched on by various writers (*see* Burns, 1981; Forester, 1980; Jones, 1980), usually in connection with labour displacement, but it has not been discussed in depth or widely applied. I shall adopt these labels to present contrasting perspectives though, as I indicate, they must be used with care as writers vary as to their degrees of optimism/pessimism, and some are optimistic in one sense but pessimistic in another. No writer *wholly* subscribes to either position, and one should not think of two separate, mutually opposed camps so much as a continuum ranging from one extreme to the other, containing various viewpoints in between (rather like the left/right divide in politics or the urban/rural distinction in geography). This provides us with a useful 'conceptual clothes line' on which to peg the wide range of contributions to the new technology debate, and for further clarification I shall introduce additional labels as different issues are discussed.

As regards the pessimists, it must be stressed at the outset that their pessimism can take different forms, and for convenience I sub-divide them into various groups. The central concerns of each are somewhat different, and we need to consider them at descending levels. The extreme pessimistic position would presumably be one that totally rejects any human use of technology, and no one seriously subscribes to this, though some believe we have allowed our world to become too 'technology oriented' and reject the general notion that technological advancement is somehow synonymous with progress. Their attacks, however, would be directed less at new information technology (which is not atmospherically polluting or a great guzzler of natural resources) than at other forms (e.g. nuclear power) and, consequently, our discussion is not over-concerned with this first level. Of greater importance for our purposes are those writers who concentrate, not so much on the technology itself — indeed, they are not particularly opposed to the technology — but are wary as to how it will be applied and controlled in a capitalist economy where private commercial interests predominate. Their focus is therefore more at the societal than the global level. These writers see the diffusion of micro-technology as part of the continuing process of rationalization and the industrial revolution, and would include those of a Marxist persuasion (e.g. Braverman) who are critical of industrial capitalism, and see new information technology as a further exploiting tool for the ruling bourgeois class. They view the process as deterministic — i.e. social controls are bound to increase and will result in a progressive degradation of work — and such a situation can only be rectified by total transformation of the existing social and economic order. Within the confines of capitalism, this viewpoint remains highly pessimistic. A deviation on this, however, is a view that holds that while the capitalist system has to maintain this rationalization process, the technology itself is neutral, and thus through conscious political and institutional action (e.g. through trade unions) people can shape its effects. This group of writers (e.g. Cooley, 1980; Jenkins and Sherman, 1979; Benson and Lloyd, 1983) may be equally disenchanted with many facets of capitalism, but they allow for an element of choice, and offer some degree of optimism within their overall pessimistic scenario. Consequently they are slightly further to the centre of our continuum. Moving further along, there are other writers who, while not necessarily opposed to the technology (or even to capitalism), are pessimistic as to the outcome if certain political policies are adopted. These writers place even greater emphasis on choice for they stress the considerable variation between societies and show how technology can be applied in many different ways. This level of pessimism therefore believes that more acceptable outcomes *can* be achieved within existing institutional arrangements, and would include those who are critical of certain policies, such as those of the Conservative government in Britain.

This sub-dividing process can of course be extended further. For instance, one might be pessimistic over how new technology is being introduced into a particular firm (or even by a particular manager) while remaining optimistic in other respects. A growing number of writers believe that it is here, at the micro, organizational level that analysis should concentrate, for they are wary of suggestions that new technology has particular universal effects — either for good or for bad. They too focus more on strategies than the technology itself and advocate a case-study based, 'contingency approach' (e.g. Child, 1984; Piercy *et al.*, 1984). These writers bring us to the centre of our continuum, for they reject a wholly optimistic or pessimistic position; argue that every application is unique; focus at the organizational level; stress the neutrality of technology; and emphasize human choice.

As we have discussed these different forms of pessimism and moved towards the centre of our continuum, so it should be noted that the level of analysis has descended (from the global to the particular); the element of optimism has increased; and greater emphasis has been placed on human choice. This allows us to extend our continuum somewhat, and the conceptual framework the reader should keep in mind is shown in Fig. 2.2. I would not wish to overstate this model, or suggest that all contributions can be neatly fitted into it, for the continuum is not made up of straight

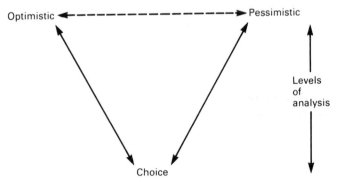

Figure 2.2   The optimistic/pessimistic continuum

lines so much as messy squiggles — blurred here, sharp there — but it does provide a useful, general framework for classifying the different viewpoints. It also reminds us that a particular writer might be optimistic in one sense, but pessimistic in another, and we must be clear as to the level and in which context a label is being applied.

Discussion of the broad question over whether we should reappraise our whole attitude to work, and our uses of technology, is deferred until Chapter 9. In the other chapters, most of the debate centres at the 'middle levels of pessimism' — i.e. with those commentators who are critical of our existing capitalist order or towards certain policies that are being introduced — and consideration of the British context is particularly strong in Chapters 3, 7 and 8.

Technology as a social product

Whereas the optimists start with technology, the pessimists start with society and its power structures, and consider technology more as a social product. They see technology principally as the *dependent* variable, resulting from various social, political and economic forces. Their overriding fear is that technology will be allowed to develop on terms dictated by power-holders, to the detriment and exclusion of the mass of the population. To varying degrees, they fear greater control and surveillance — by particular countries, companies and social groups; mass unemployment; the misuse of valuable natural resources; growing inequalities in wealth and power; and further depersonalization of life and work.

Those writers who are critical of industrial capitalism particularly reject the convergence writers' suggestion that technology somehow 'spontaneously emerges' to independently determine the form a particular society takes. On the contrary, they argue that technologies are found because they are sought; and are adopted, designed, released, applied and controlled by those trying to protect their own interests. Technology is not snatched from thin air, but reflects the way we live and work, and if we lived and worked differently, then technology would reflect it. Dickson (1974) and Reinecke (1984) expound this view which holds that we live in a capitalist (as opposed to an industrial) society, one based on exploitation and conflict rather than convergence and consensus, and divided between those who hold economic and political power and those who do not.

Braverman argues that under capitalism, labour power is geared to the creation of profit rather than the satisfaction of man's needs, and technology is used to enhance this. The division of labour takes on a particular form, and far from allowing workers to *choose* to sub-divide tasks among themselves (the social division of labour) it is now used to assign workers to specific tasks (the manufacturing division of labour). This means workers become incapable of carrying out a complete production process and that through the increased use of technology, jobs are simplified (deskilled) and cheapened so that capitalists can employ unskilled as opposed to skilled labour, and use machines to replace human strength and skill. Instead of justifying the division of labour in terms of 'preserving scarce skills' — as Bell would claim in the case of his skilled technocrats — Braverman argues that its main appeal is to provide cheap labour for unskilled jobs. In that this view is critical of the status quo and apprehensive as to how new technology might be used, it tends to find favour on the political left.

Taylorism

A key factor in this process, along with scientific and technological development, is the application of the scientific management principles of Frederick Taylor (1911). The essence of scientific management, or Taylorism, was that managers should study jobs 'scientifically' — in terms of operations, tools, speed etc. — to determine and impose one 'best' method for each task which then replaces all others. As Taylor himself explained: 'In my system, the workman is told minutely what he is to do and how he is to do it, and any improvement he makes upon the instructions given to him is fatal to success.'

The gains, according to Taylor, would be that management and workforce could each concentrate on what suited them best; problems of worker slacking and managerial incompetence could be overcome; and all would benefit financially through higher wages or profits. As Taylor put it: 'The principal object of management should be to secure the maximum prosperity for the employer, coupled with the maximum prosperity of each employee.' He called for a 'mental revolution' in which: 'Both sides should take their eyes off the division of the surplus as the all important matter and together turn their attention towards increasing the size of the surplus.'

The application of Taylor's principles certainly produced far greater output and wealth, but Braverman argues that it also permitted managers to monopolize all existing knowledge and dissociate the labour process from the skills of the workers. Workers are now paid to work, not to think, and the conception and execution of work become divorced from each other. The worker no longer uses his initiative; is forbidden from 'conceiving' the job to be undertaken; and merely executes the task in the swiftest possible manner according to set instructions. Work is deskilled in terms of knowledge, responsibility and discretion.

The impetus is thus for employers to make jobs as simple and precise as possible, and this is assisted by the installation of machines designed to incorporate the manual and mental skills previously held by workers. This also had implications for factory organization, and the likes of Henry Ford extended Taylor's ideas through the development of assembly-line production. Tasks now required very few skills as workers became mere appendages to machines; machines which ultimately might totally replace workers and deny them the opportunity to work at all.

Stages of technological development

This view of technological development proceeds through certain stages in which those who apply the technology aim to replace human skill, effort and control with mechanical devices. We can classify this process as follows:

1. Mechanized manual production — in which tools/machines are used by skilled workers to perform tasks.
2. Mechanized production — in which work is performed by machines partly operated by workers.
3. Integrated mechanized production — in which the whole production cycle is performed by machines, controlled and regulated by workers.
4. Automated production — in which tasks are performed by machines that are checked by workers.
5. Integrated automated production — in which the production process is totally automated and human intervention is not required.

Seen through this model, the assembly line is a transitional technology which can now be replaced through microelectronics with the fully automated factory. Technology becomes increasingly reliable and incorporates automatic monitoring and fault-correcting devices which dispose of virtually all human skills.

In a sense, therefore, Braverman envisages a society similar to Bell — in which technology performs our various tasks and provides for our basic needs — but the means of achieving this end are totally different. He rejects the notion that there is some evolutionary 'logic of industrialism' that results in a particular form of society and, while he would agree that in a society based on cooperation and trust, new technology *could* have a liberating rather than a degrading effect, he sees little sign of this happening under capitalism. For Braverman, the nature of work and production technology are still the products of class relations: capitalism remains very much intact, and without fundamental changes new technology will simply reinforce the status quo.

CONCLUSION

I have presented different perspectives on the technology–society interface and shall shortly relate these to a more detailed discussion of new information technology. For purposes of clarification, the different emphases of the two main camps — both of which acknowledge considerable change — are summarized in Table 2.1.

In order to point up the differences in the perspectives, my discussion has, necessarily, been broad and simplified. I repeat that we are not talking of mono-causal relationships: this is never the case, and no writer in either camp subscribes to a simple-minded determinism. Our models are 'ideal type abstractions' at polar ends of a continuum, which hopefully will assist our appreciation of the various viewpoints that range in between.

In concluding this chapter, I should add that on some occasions the two camps seem to be talking past each other, for they tend to focus on separate issues; adopt different time-scales; and sometimes use the same labels to mean different things. For instance, though Bell talks of 'revolution', many would criticize his use of the word for he applies it in a narrow, largely *technological* sense. If we consider the *means* by which the 'end' of his post-industrial society comes about, his approach is not 'revolutionary' at all, but strongly 'evolutionary'. Critics would question why, when the first industrial revolution clearly involved so much

Table 2.1 Characteristics of the contrasting perspectives

	Optimistic view	*Pessimistic view*
Society	Industrial	Capitalist
Technology	Neutral product	Social product
Technological focus	Invention	Innovation
Technological change	Revolutionary	Evolutionary
Social structure	Elite (meritocratic technocrats)	Class (economic owners)
Changes to social structure	Convergence	Polarization
Social relations	Consensus	Conflict
Nature of work	Reskilling	Deskilling
State	Pluralist	Unitary
Political orientation	Conservative	Radical

upheaval and class conflict, this present revolution should provide increasing harmony and consensus. They would particularly question whether new social and occupational classes have emerged, the last of Deane's features. Even if technocrats are more important, pessimists would claim that the capitalists are still very much in control, and society characterized by exploitation and conflict. Critics would insist that any true revolution has to involve a change in the mode of economic production and a shift in the make-up of the ruling class. New technology may be revolutionary in terms of what it can do, but it is a product of existing society rather than a catalyst for change. Thus a term like 'micro revolution' is acceptable to both camps, but the pessimists would question a 'new industrial revolution'.

There is also an important difference with regard to time-scale. Those who question whether new technology will in itself fundamentally enhance the nature of work in capitalist society (i.e. the pessimists) tend to restrict their remarks to the short term, and in most instances prefer to focus at lower levels of analysis. The optimistic convergence writers, on the other hand, seem happy to indulge in long-term global speculation.

Having established the differing perspectives, I shall now apply them to a discussion of the human effects of new information technology; particularly in relation to employment, the workplace, citizenship and the home.

CHAPTER THREE

Employment

The issue in the new technology debate that has aroused most controversy is probably that of labour displacement. That unemployment is already a serious problem for many industrialized nations cannot be disputed. By the start of 1985 it had risen to 3 340 958 in Britain and 13 million for the EEC as a whole; 13.9 per cent and 11.6 per cent of the respective workforces. This represented a fivefold increase since the mid-1970s and despite various explanations and proposed solutions, it still shows little sign of abating. Many would even argue that the official figures — because of the way they are collated — underestimate the true situation. To what extent is new technology the cause of this, and should we expect the situation to worsen rather than improve in future? Interestingly, this discussion has been more widespread in Britain and Europe than, say, Japan and the United States (perhaps because we have recently experienced greater unemployment) and, consequently, this chapter will largely concentrate on the British experience. Is the microchip the great 'job-killer' or alternatively, as some would claim, does it herald a much-needed stimulus for our economy, to carry us out of recession? It is at the same time presented as the panacea for all our industrial troubles, and as a force that will destroy work as we know it and divisively polarize society between those in regular, highly skilled employment and those with no work at all.

We can immediately divide between optimists and pessimists, and apply our continuum to consider the range of views. Towards one extreme are the 'ultra-pessimists' — for instance, Marxist writers who see new technology inevitably leading to higher unemployment, for this is a recurring feature of capitalism.

Technology has always been used to replace labour power: microelectronics will be no different; and many more will be unemployed in an increasingly polarized society. Optimists, on the other hand, argue that labour-saving technology is nothing new; that it has never by itself increased unemployment in the long term; that we have survived structural change before; and that microelectronics will create wealth and boost jobs.

This is to simplify and set the debate in broad terms. In one sense, *everyone* is a pessimist, for there is little dispute that new information technology will displace certain tasks, but the argument hinges on whether it will also revitalize the economy to the extent that it creates new areas of work and higher employment levels overall. The pessimists concentrate on job *loss*, while the optimists stress job *creation*. We are therefore dealing with two separate issues: whether technology *causes* labour displacement, and whether, in the long term, it *results* in it. Though related, the two are not the same thing, and one can accept the first while rejecting the second. In other words, we first need to establish the existing sectors most likely to be affected by new technology and, secondly, to consider whether the effects of the technology itself could be such as to stimulate fresh jobs in new areas. This is a distinction between 'process innovation', where old tasks are done in new ways, and 'product innovation', where new markets, goods, services and, thereby, jobs are created. The first of these is far easier to determine and, as we shall see, there is general agreement that jobs in certain sectors could be at risk. However, this need not mean society experiences unemployment in *aggregate* terms, and this is the main issue for debate.

THE PRESENT CLIMATE

Any discussion on the effects of new information technology on employment must be set in a broad context. Firstly, it must be stressed that new technology is emerging against a backcloth of world recession, and in Britain within the framework of ostensibly monetarist government policies. If employment was high, then we probably wouldn't spend so much time worrying about the effects of new technology, but then if it was high we presumably would not (if Kondratiev is correct) be thinking of installing new technology anyway. The context therefore colours the position that different people adopt. The pessimists are generally critical of government policies which they believe have intensified unemployment; they insist that the continuance of such policies will further exacerbate the situation; and they believe new technology could play an important role in this process. The optimists, on the other hand, believe that unemployment is a current world problem; that the government is right in trying to hold down inflation; that this is the only way of providing secure jobs in the long term; and that new technology can assist rather than hinder this process. Each side therefore tends to engage in 'self-fulfilling prophecies' and there is no way one can say one is right and the other wrong.

Secondly, new technology is merely one factor among many that may affect employment patterns. While technological change invariably creates transitional unemployment, this will vary considerably according to the underlying growth rate of a country's economy, its international competitiveness, the global energy situation, government policies, changes in the labour force etc., and consequently the same technology can have very different effects in different countries. In addition, these various factors become so intertwined that it is impossible to extrapolate one as an independent variable and measure its precise impact. To talk of the effect of new technology in isolation from other influences is rather like talking about the impact of a new centre-forward on a football team without any reference to the others who play alongside him.

Nor should it be thought that a rise in unemployment necessarily means a fall in employment. A key factor in Britain over the past two decades has been the growth in the labour force due to the fact that (a) more women have wanted work, (b) the baby boom of the 1950s and 1960s created more school-leavers, and (c) less people were retiring as fewer were born during the First World War. We now have a higher proportion of women in the labour force (along with Denmark) than any other EEC country, and as many women now *expect* to work, they register as unemployed if made redundant, thus boosting the figures. Whereas women only made up 23 per cent of Europe's unemployed in 1970, the figure was 42 per cent by 1984. This helps explain why unemployment has continued to rise despite the arrival of new jobs: in 1984, 250 000 new jobs were created, but unemployment rose because 480 000 more entered the workforce. By 1985, Britain could boast a record labour force of 26 450 000 and was the only European country to have created

600 000 more jobs in the previous two years, but still unemployment rose towards 4 million.

Economists on the political right — who we can label 'monetarist' — suggest that British employment legislation plays a big part in increasing unemployment in that it makes it too difficult for employers to 'hire and fire'. They also suggest that increases in social benefit rates have increased dole queues for they have acted as a disincentive for people to seek work. Unlike the American system, where support is granted for only a few months after which it runs out, our flat-rate system is seen as providing a minimum out-of-work income available indefinitely even to people not seriously looking for a job. The argument is that 'effective demand' should regulate employment, and that if there is an over-supply of labour then wages should fall, thus making it profitable for employers to hire more workers. Many leading monetarists believe that a 10 per cent cut in wages would provide a 10 per cent increase in jobs, and are therefore critical of trade union demands which they claim keep wages artificially high, result in inflation and ultimately provide fewer jobs for others. This view aims to encourage perfect markets in which employers can offer jobs 'at the right price' and people are encouraged to go in search of them.

THE IMPACT OF NEW INFORMATION TECHNOLOGY

The chip therefore further compounds an already highly complex and contentious situation. As I have stressed, it is impossible to determine the precise amount of labour displacement attributable to new technology, particularly in Britain where take-up to date has generally been slow, and when economists adopt contrasting perspectives. There is a wide gulf between those who expect unemployment to rise by many more millions and those who predict an eventual increase in jobs. Just as economists vary in their emphasis on particular causal factors, and how they collate and interpret statistics, so they divide over their predictions of future work patterns.

It is understandable that the chip has aroused concern in Britain for we are already experiencing a serious unemployment problem, while fears have been intensified by the astonishing development of the technology itself, which makes people wary of suggestions that this is 'just another technology'. It is hardly surprising that towards the end of the 1970s a 'pessimistic viewpoint' emerged regarding the employment effects of microelectronics.

The pessimistic view

This view argues that the net effect of new technology will be to create an overall decline in job opportunities and thus lead to large-scale and possibly permanent unemployment problems. New information technology is seen as qualitatively different from earlier forms for it significantly replaces work by brain as well as by hand. While in the first industrial revolution, workers displaced from the land could move into the fast-growing towns, in the present situation, those displaced from factories and offices seem likely to have nowhere to go as any new industries will be highly automated and only employ minimal workforces. In the short term, lack of innovation and investment may hold back the effects, but in time they will become significant. The scale of these effects will of course be influenced by governmental policies — and, it is argued, they will be far greater if monetarist policies are pursued than if public investment is expanded — but overall the outcome will be one of substantial job loss.

This pessimistic view gained momentum in the late 1970s through the likes of Clive Jenkins' and Barrie Sherman's much-publicized book *The Collapse of Work* in which they argued that Britain was faced with 'Hobson's choice' over new information technology:

> Remain as we are, reject the new technologies, and we face unemployment of up to 5.5 million by the end of the century. Embrace the new technologies, accept the challenge, and we end up with unemployment of about 5 million.

They suggest that if we do not embrace new technology we will suffer unemployment for we will cease to remain competitive as an industrialized nation, but similarly, if we do embrace it we will experience job loss for microelectronics will perform our necessary tasks — hence 'work collapses'. They argue that of these alternatives the latter is preferable for it allows us to remain a wealthy, advanced nation. Their work involved an industry-by-industry analysis of likely job effects and they suggest that occupations can be divided into three basic groups:

(a) Occupations that will hardly be affected at all: farm labourers, trawlermen, general labourers, top management, leisure employees.

(b) Occupations that will be minimally affected: security and protection specialists, professional staffs, catering, hairdressing and other personal services, education, health and welfare services, construction and mining.

(c) Occupations that will be considerably affected: handling and storing, clerical work, manufacturing workers, repair workers, middle management, foremen, financial and 'information' employees.

Among manpower economists, the Science Policy Research Unit (SPRU) of Sussex University believe that with the increasing demand for jobs, Britain can by 1990, expect an unemployment figure of around 5 million. This will result from demographic trends; the relatively poor performance of the UK economy; the slower growth rate of the world economy as a whole; and new technology. Technological change will affect employment in *both* the manufacturing and service sectors, which could create a polarization between (a) a large pool of unemployable labour and (b) a small group of highly skilled and highly-paid workers in technological employment. To date, the displacement effects may not have been significant — because take-up in Britain has generally been slow — but they believe that long term the consequences could be very severe indeed.

At Cambridge University, in work less specifically directed at new technology, the Economic Policy Group have similarly predicted that unemployment could reach anything from 4 to 7 million by the end of the 1980s, depending on government policies. If unemployment did reach the level of 6 or 7 million, it would present central government, industrial management and the trade unions with an enormous task. Due to the unprecedented combination of demographic factors, the workforce can be expected to rise significantly up to 1990 (though the situation should go into reverse after that), and 300 000 new jobs will be needed just to keep unemployment at its present level. This would require a growth rate in excess of 5 per cent per annum, a tall order given the post-war performance of the British economy.

This depressing (some would say alarmist) outlook has even received support from the National Economic Development Council (NEDC) which supposedly reflects the collective views of government, industrial management and the trade unions. In 1982, their policy for the UK electronics industry suggested that people could well lose jobs to new machines, and their report on the effects of technology on the distributive trades argued that the idea that mass unemployment is temporary is 'dangerously false'. They question political cant about restoring employment and suggest that, at best, employment will do no more than remain stable up to 1987.

Case studies

There is a vast amount of case study material from both the manufacturing and office sectors to support the pessimists' claims, though to repeat, it is often hard to disentangle the effects of automation from those of the recession. In traditional manufacturing, many companies have drastically cut labour and there seems little indication that this sector will provide the springboard for new jobs in the future. At Rolls Royce, Derby, three men per shift are now producing what once required thirty; Plessey have reduced their Liverpool workforce by 825 over two years as they expand production of digital telephone exchanges; Austin Rover have cut their workforce by 20 000 and invested heavily in automation; GKN have reduced their UK workforce by 35 000 in the past five years, etc., etc. In a study of the effects of new technology on 163 workplaces, the Labour Research Department found in 1982 that job losses had occurred in a third of the cases. Between 1979 and 1985, employment in the manufacturing sector fell by over 25 per cent to less than 5.5 million — an overall drop of 3 million since 1961 — and the signs are that this will continue.

The high technology industries themselves should generate many new jobs, but whether in sufficient quantity to replace all those that are lost seems doubtful, as there is every indication that they will prove capital-, rather than labour-intensive. Ironically, in the computer and electronics industry itself — which has rapidly expanded — the numbers in manufacturing fell by over 10 000 during the 1970s, and the same is happening in telecommunications where System X will eventually require only 4 per cent of the present workforce to produce it and virtually no one to run it. Employment in telecommunications, the manufacture of cash registers and weighing machines, and TV production all fell during the 1970s, and not just in Britain. Philips of Holland, a major electrical company employing nearly half a million world-wide, predict that even allowing for a 3 per cent growth rate it will be 56 per cent overmanned by 1990, while in Japan workers in TV production were cut by 50 per cent during the 1970s though output rose 25 per cent.

In the office sphere — identified by Jenkins and Sherman as a key sector — the evidence is equally alarming. Bradford City Council reduced its staff in one sector from forty-four to twenty-two with the introduction of nine word processors, which provided a productivity increase of 19 per cent and an estimated annual saving of some £59 000. The British Standards Institution created a centralized specialist word-processing department when it installed ten IBM word processors, and cut the number of typists and secretaries by a third. At the Provident Financial, when three IBM machines were introduced into the central typing pool, the full-time staff was cut from twenty-seven to seventeen, and the part-time staff from thirteen to three. The expanding Halifax Building Society moved from automatic typewriters to sixteen IBM word processors, trebled its workload, but took on no extra staff. Littlewoods, the mail-order firm, introduced a computer and cut 600 jobs during 1985. And so on. Ursula Huws (1982) found in her study of forty workplaces in West Yorkshire that new technology was particularly likely to hit women's jobs. While 60 per cent of the workplaces employed more men, only in 17 per cent of cases were more men's jobs affected. In one mail-order office, computerization reduced the clerical staff from 1000 to 550.

The response of white-collar trade unions has largely been pessimistic. The Association of Scientific, Technical and Managerial Staffs (ASTMS) has warned that almost two out of every three employees are in occupations at risk, with clerical workers particularly vulnerable. It has forecast that 3.9 million information workers could lose their jobs by 1991. The Association of Professional, Executive, Clerical and Computer Staffs (APEX) conducted a survey in the West Midlands in 1984 and argued that for every job created by new information technology, fifty would eventually disappear, and that as only 4 per cent of offices could be said to be fully computerized, the revolution was only just beginning. In West Germany it has been estimated in the Siemens study that office employment could fall by 40 per cent (2 million jobs) by 1990, and in France the Nora report of 1977 estimated a 30 per cent drop in banking and insurance staff by the same date.

The optimistic view

In the light of such depressing forecasts, it may seem surprising that some should take a totally opposite line; but this is indeed the case. The optimists concede that new technology may cause some labour displacement, for this has always been the consequence of technological innovation, but they reject the idea that it will *result* in higher unemployment overall.

They began to present their case in the early 1980s, largely as a response to the pessimists, and this is hardly surprising for without the promulgations of Jenkins and Sherman and others, they would have seen no need to raise the issue at all. Being optimists, they see little cause for concern regarding new technology: technological change is a continuous feature of industrial development, and there is as much reason to suppose that it stimulates employment opportunities as depresses them. Employment in the railways, chemicals and metal manufacture all rose significantly following technological innovation, and there were actually more professional musicians, not less, after the arrival of the domestic record player! To say that we are moving into a world in which there will not be enough to do because technology carries out our basic tasks is to the optimists to consider employment solely in terms of producing the goods and services we *presently* need. These are not fixed, and though displacement may occur in some areas, fresh opportunities should emerge in others. Optimists therefore incline to the view that the effect on jobs will ultimately be qualitative rather than quantitative. Employment patterns will certainly change as new jobs replace old, but this should be slow, giving the economy time to re-adjust.

Japan is often quoted as the shining example to disprove the pessimists' foreboding. Though that society has invested massively in new information technology, unemployment has been kept to under 3 per cent, and five times as many people are now employed in areas such as marketing and production planning. Just as the Luddites were misguided in 1811 when they smashed up the machines they feared would destroy their jobs, and the 'prophets of doom' in the 1950s were proved wrong when they claimed the first mainframe computers would result in unemployment so, it is argued, pessimists overstate the likely effects of microelectronics.

One of the best-known optimists is Patrick Minford (1984) who rejects the view that new technology will destroy jobs and maintains that the long-term outlook for employment could be bright if government helped rather than hindered fluidity in the labour market. He suggests that unemployment will fall (as it did before) when we come through recession and dismisses the idea that unemployment is becoming a permanent feature of industrial society as 'rubbish'. Just as in the past new jobs were created when technology displaced old ones, so the same thing will happen again. As a 'market-oriented' economist, he views technology as uniform and dismisses the suggestion that particular forms may have special effects. He believes market forces can deal with unemployment and that these work best if not interfered with by government. He accepts some degree of unemployment as inevitable (frictional) but argues that cyclical unemployment is largely determined by global economic forces and will only fall when we come through recession.

In similar vein, the Institute for Employment Research at Warwick University suggest that while around 340 000 jobs could be displaced by 1990, this loss will be more than compensated for by the creation of 420 000 new ones. Many of these will not be directly in innovating sectors, but will result from the knock-on effects in non-innovating sectors, e.g. construction. The argument of the optimists is that if human wants remain to be satisfied, then higher demand will call forth the production of new goods and services. Yesterday's luxuries become today's necessities, and people's expectations rise. In the 1930s many people demanded little more than a waterproof home, protection from major diseases, sufficient food and a steady job: there was no demand for television performers as the technology did not exist.

This optimistic line appears in many reports from various government advisory bodies. For instance, in its report to the Cabinet in 1980, the Advisory Council for Applied Research and Development (ACARD) advocated the necessity for immediately embracing microelectronics but maintained that there was no certainty this would lead to increasing unemployment. Presenting the traditional argument that economic growth leads to greater employment, it adopted an optimistic standpoint and suggested that:

If new technology leads to an increase in market share, there is generally an increase in employment opportunities. The labour resources made available by reductions in employment in some manufacturing sectors will provide the opportunity for rapid expansion in quite different sectors.

In its 1979 report, the Department of Employment (DEP) Manpower Study Group concluded that

> ...the overall employment effect is virtually impossible to gauge. However, past empirical work suggests that, in the long run, technological change has been beneficial to both output and employment ... the employment implications in quantitative terms are likely to be insignificant. (Sleigh et al., 1979)

Arguing from case study material (as global figures can easily be inaccurate), they suggest that in practice few companies are taking advantage of the new technological devices that are now theoretically possible, and that labour displacement effects can easily be exaggerated. As regards the service sector, they predict that the effects of technological change could be to reduce clerical jobs over five to ten years, but also create new skills. However, change will be slow, and the all-electronic, paperless office is still many years away in reality. For many firms it is the shortage of typists, rather than any wish to remove those they have, that prompts them to buy expensive word processors.

Virginia Williams (1984) of the DEP's Economics Division also maintains that the direct effects of new technology on jobs have to date been small — probably accounting for no more than 5 per cent of the jobs lost during the recession of the early 1980s — and that labour displacement still primarily depends on competitiveness. She expects the rate of technological diffusion to rise considerably in future but feels the labour displacement effects could remain less than many commentators expect.

Perhaps not surprisingly, just as many trade unions adopt a pessimistic line, so the Confederation of British Industry (CBI) takes an optimistic stance. In its 1980 report, it concludes that the only permanent solution to unemployment is to create viable jobs in new and expanding industries, and that microelectronics could help in this process. It sees the impact of new technology on unemployment as being uneven, and though some sectors could decline, fresh areas for work will emerge. The report does, however, acknowledge that with 2 million more workers entering the labour market up to 1991 it might not prove possible to absorb all of them immediately.

	1978 (%)	2000 (%)
Farmers	3.2	3.4
Labourers	4.9	5.5
Sales Workers	6.6	6.5
Managers	9.5	7.2
Professionals	15.6	19.8
Operatives	15.7	16.5
Craftsmen	13.3	15.0
Service Workers	12.4	14.7
Clerical Workers	17.8	11.4
Miscellaneous	1.0	0.0
	100.0	100.0

Figure 3.1   Predicted make-up of the United States labour force, 2000

The Nobel prize-winning economist Wassily Leontief (1985) of New York University has suggested that far from micro-technology displacing workers, it is more likely that there will not be enough workers to operate all the machines we will want. In that he believes job creation will overshadow job loss, Leontief might be termed a 'super-optimist'. He concedes that there will be a dramatic fall in office workers (but not production workers) and argues that this will be compensated for by a rise in craftsmen, labourers, operatives, service workers and, in particular, professionals (Fig. 3.1).

Blue-collar workers may lose their present jobs, but they will be rehired in growing industries producing equipment for the techno-logical revolution. As regards America, his projections suggest that *too many* jobs will be generated by 2000 for what is likely to be the size of the labour force. If unemployment does stay high, he suggests it will be for reasons other than technology, such as the deflationary response of government to pay claims etc. There are differences, of course, between the United States and Britain (e.g. they have more farmers) but Leontief believes the same broad changes will occur in all industrialized economies. His overriding message is that the faster we adapt ourselves to the new technology, the sooner we will be able to experience high living standards and low unemployment.

The long-term optimistic view
In between the two views we have considered so far are a third group of writers who I shall label long-term optimists (or, if you

prefer, short-term pessimists) who are located closer to the centre of our continuum. This includes those who adopt a Keynesian view; favour a 'mixed economy'; and believe government should play a key role through public investment in stimulating economic activity. They are optimistic over long-term job creation and believe that employment consequences are manageable within present institutional arrangements — if, of course, appropriate policies are adopted. Their pessimism is therefore more short term and relates to the specific policies being pursued by the present government, i.e. they are 'lower level' pessimists. Their scenario suggests that new technology will cause considerable displacement in certain sectors, but this should prove temporary, and though the rate of change will greatly depend on inter-related factors such as government policies, energy costs and bank interest rates, there is every reason to expect that, long term, overall employment levels will rise.

This view is well represented in the work of Tom Stonier (1982, 1984) who maintains that jobs in traditional manufacturing industries will be removed by new technology and that the new hi-tech industries will not provide new ones in sufficient numbers to balance the displacement. He predicts that by the turn of the century only 10 per cent of the labour force will be needed to provide our material needs. Of the remainder (if they are not unemployed), 10 per cent will be in finance and commerce, 5–10 per cent will be in leisure industries, 25–30 per cent in health, police and other social services, and 40 per cent in what he terms the 'knowledge industry'. This is close to Daniel Bell, who suggests that people-to-machine jobs, in both factory and office, will decline to be replaced by people-to-people jobs. Information now becomes a more important resource than land, labour or capital, and just as technology allowed people to move from the land to the factory, so now it allows them to move from the factory to the new service sectors.

To Jenkins and Sherman, these 'information' jobs are equally ripe for automation; but Stonier shares Minford's optimism that they could help create fresh employment opportunities for the 1990s. Where they differ, however, is over the particular policies they believe will bring this about. Stonier is Keynesian in that he advocates a major *governmental* role in job creation, not just in infrastructure projects but also in 'human capital' through the expansion of such areas as education and health care. The 'caring industries' could be improved by decreasing the client/staff ratio, and rather than destroying employment, should have an almost infinite capacity, Stonier argues, for providing work. This 'social policy response', as he terms it, would encourage projects that had a clearly positive impact on the country's productivity and would yield revenue to the government either directly or indirectly. Government's role would therefore be to help the private sector produce wealth, and also expand public sector employment.

POLITICAL RESPONSES

The view of the present government is strongly optimistic; the *laissez-faire* arguments of Patrick Minford and others have become economic orthodoxy. Market forces will deal with any threat to employment, and these operate best when not interfered with by government. Microelectronics is merely a further stage of technological development and should be welcomed as a means of saving labour costs, which helps keep inflation down, makes manufacturing industry more competitive and — in the long term — boosts employment. As former Information Technology Minister Kenneth Baker put it, it is not automation, but the *failure* to automate, that puts jobs at risk: it is a case of 'automate or liquidate'.

The Labour Party seems to correspond more to the position of Stonier. The party is not 'anti-new technology' and does not believe that it will necessarily result in long-term labour displacement, but is concerned that it may cause considerable short-term damage, particularly under Conservative policies. In its 1982 report, the Labour Party science and technology group argued that science and technology are not bound to cause the collapse of work but could be vital to the restoration of full employment. Technology, however, is not the key factor so much as economic policy, and they stress that '...It is vital that rapid technological change takes place in a context of sustained economic growth so that the large productivity gains made possible in some sectors are absorbed by the expansion of employment in others' (*Microelectronics*, 1980).

The Labour Party is Keynesian, in that it maintains that the public sector offers considerable scope for direct job' creation. Britain should invest in the national infrastructure — roads, railways, sewers, water services etc. — and develop the necessary facilities — fibre-optic cable, satellites, home terminals, appropriate workplaces etc. — to accommodate the new information technology. Secondly, government should invest in the labour-intensive, welfare industries — as Stonier suggests — to provide new jobs as well as to improve the quality and coverage of the services themselves. In 1984 the party called for a £30 billion, five-year public investment programme in roads, sewers, schools and hospitals so that the reduction of unemployment could be given top priority. Similarly, the SDP/Liberal Alliance has demanded an increase of £5 billion a year, including a £1 billion programme for public construction and other infrastructure projects.

Support for reflationary policies (albeit to a lesser extent) has also come from the ranks of the government's own supporters, including a number of Conservative MPs, as well as the CBI and other industrialists. The so-called 'wets' have called for the economy to be reflated by anything up to £6 billion, and for an expansion of public works and an incomes policy. Sir Ian Gilmour, MP has argued that new information technology is not creating employment, mainly because it doesn't get the same government support as in other countries, but secondly, because domestic demand has not been created at the 'macro' level to generate a strong home base for the hi-tech industries. Our surplus from North Sea oil has been used to fund dole queues rather than provide infrastructure changes; investment remains at a low level; and unemployment continues to rise. Similar criticisms have come from Edward Heath, Francis Pym and Peter Walker. In 1985, many of these ideas found expression in the formation of an all-party Employment Institute, including various politicians, former civil servants, trade unionists and journalists, all critical of the government line.

The common theme in all these arguments is that the government should be prepared to borrow in order to invest in the national infrastructure to provide new jobs and equip society for technological change. This is now so vital that it cannot solely be left to the private sector and, as in other countries, government must play a dominant role. The government reply is that we have been down this road many times before and it always leads to inflation.

Ultimately, the whole issue depends on one's view of how efficiently and quickly markets work. If they work perfectly (or could be made to work perfectly), then unemployment cannot persist for any great length of time, irrespective of any 'shocks' to the system such as microelectronics, oil crises or whatever. If, on the other hand, prices and wages are inflexible, and supplies and demands only respond to changes slowly (as appears to be the case in Britain), then imbalances such as unemployment can persist. Once again, therefore, we come back to perspectives and to reminding ourselves that how we look at something largely determines what we see. The monetarists approximate more closely to the view that the government should disengage itself from direct economic activity and allow market systems to work, while Keynesians insist they will never work effectively without governmental stimulus.

RECONCILING THE DIFFERENT APPROACHES

In this chapter, I have collated a wide range of contributions to the employment debate into three main camps: the pessimists, optimists and long-term optimists. All agree that displacement in certain sectors (e.g. the office) is virtually certain, but while the pessimists believe this will result in greater job losses overall, the long-term optimists maintain it should only be for the short term, while the optimists claim that new jobs will replace old. (The super-optimists even believe we shall eventually create more jobs than we can fill.)

To the layman — who up to now perhaps had some faith in economics — much of this must seem puzzling. With such disparity between those who predict unemployment possibly rising to 7 million and those who expect greater employment as a result of microelectronics, one can see why economics is termed the 'dismal science'.

All is not lost, however, for one could claim that the different schools are not so far apart as they might appear. In the first place, because the various contributors adopt different perspectives, they also employ very different methodological approaches. The pessimists base most of their work on macro-economic models which, critics claim, insufficiently allow for the wide range of extraneous variables. Suggestions that microelectronics can cause X million unemployed can, by themselves, be very misleading, for regional variations, female employment and population trends are just some of the secondary factors that must be taken into account.

Pessimists can easily over-state the potential of new technology, implying it will be adopted overnight, and confusing what is possible with what is probable. In Britain the take-up has generally been slow due, many would say, to the fact that we are a relatively low-wage economy which provides little incentive for firms to invest in new, expensive techniques. Finally, critics maintain that some pessimists wish to use new technology to prove something they already believe, i.e. that the British economy is in irreversible decline and the capitalist system doomed.

As to the optimists, because they are suspicious of large-scale economic models, they prefer to employ a more 'micro' approach and focus on individual workplaces. The DEP Manpower Study Group, for example, based its work on case studies, but this too has limitations. Those firms which have invested in new technology to date tend to be more progressive and successful, and labour displacement has been avoided through their increase in market share. (At a national level, this in effect is what has happened in Japan.) In Britain they still represent a minority and should not be taken as representative in terms of labour displacement effects. As we saw earlier, one can easily quote workplace examples that argue the opposite outcome. Consequently, because of the methods they adopt, the pessimists run the risk of overstating, and the optimists understating, the likely displacement figures.

Another factor we have to consider is work time. This is not fixed, and while during the industrial revolution the average working week was as high as eighty hours, this has now fallen to forty and could fall further. Clearly, changes to the working week, longer holidays and earlier retirement could significantly alter the situation. Jenkins and Sherman certainly expect such developments in view of the displacement they predict, and talk not just of a 'shorter working week' but a 'shorter working lifetime'. They envisage far greater flexibility in working hours, sabbaticals, job changes, earlier retirement etc. But Stonier too foresees people working far shorter hours, and even arch-optimist Kenneth Baker has predicted that by 2000 most will be working a four-day week, forty weeks a year, mainly from home or in small offices or workshops.

The Labour Party too acknowledges that attitudes will have to change. While unemployment went up by millions between 1975 and 1985, overtime levels stayed the same, and work sharing and shorter work periods seem inevitable if the problem is to be resolved.

If this is so, are the various camps really that far apart from each other? After all, to say that everyone will be in work but will only work four days a week and forty weeks a year (and possibly retire at fifty) is surely not so different from saying that unemployment (with conditions unchanged) will rise to 5 million. The difference is simply in terms of how the available work is spread. Baker presumably, being an optimist, assumes that shorter working hours will 'just happen' while Jenkins and Sherman only expect it if particular policies are pursued.

Therefore, if one delves beneath the differences in emphasis — and rhetoric — one starts to identify a broad scenario that many would subscribe to. It goes something like this. Britain must adopt new technology if we wish to remain as a competitive, Western industrialized nation, but this will certainly lead to labour displacement in certain areas (e.g. the office). New areas of work will emerge as new products and services are provided and new demands arise. These will provide new wealth, but are unlikely to create sufficient jobs to balance the displacement, so what is available must be shared if those who desire work are to obtain some. Within these parameters, the scope and pace of particular changes remains problematic and this debate is considered further in Chapter 9.

CHAPTER FOUR

The Factory

In the next two chapters we move from the quantitative to the qualitative; from a consideration of the number at work to the changing nature of the work they do. There are broadly three things that can happen to people's jobs as a result of new technology: they can be eliminated, upgraded or deskilled; and having dealt with the first of these in the previous chapter, we now consider the other two.

Industries such as precision engineering, motor vehicle manufacture and printing, and service sectors such as banking and insurance, have already been substantially altered by new information technology, and the range of applications and workplaces that could ultimately be affected seems unlimited. What will the effects be? In the final analysis, every application is unique and must be viewed as such, but given that social science requires some degree of generalization to say anything at all, I shall focus on the factory and office in a broad sense and not discuss the intricacies of specific jobs in particular industries. At this level, we can observe what various writers think might occur, though I would maintain that what *does* occur will depend very much on management choice.

We again find two main schools of thought — the optimists and pessimists — as regards the likely effects of applications in the factory. The first group believe that new technology will in general enhance work — that it will 'reskill' in the sense of providing greater skill opportunities — while the latter foresee further 'deskilling' as technology downgrades factory work. In these two chapters, therefore, I often refer to the two camps as the reskilling and deskilling writers.

THE RESKILLING ARGUMENT

We saw in Chapter 2 that for Bell and the convergence writers, one of the key features of industrial society is the growth in technical skills and professional competence among the workforce. This will extend further in post-industrial society as work becomes ever more sophisticated and mechanization raises skill levels; workers require greater knowledge, particularly in science and technology; and the pace of change makes education a fundamental prerequisite. Work is therefore reskilled and upgraded as microelectronics removes drudgery and repetitiveness and releases people from boring, dirty and dangerous jobs to apply their skills to more meaningful tasks.

This view is expressed in the work of Robert Blauner (1964) who adapted Marx's concept of alienation to consider job satisfaction in various American workplaces, but saw alienation not as a consequence of private property but rather as the result of particular forms of technology. For Blauner, alienation is a 'feeling', an individual property, while for Marx it results from structural forces and is an inevitable outcome. Blauner presents four dimensions of alienation which can be best understood if contrasted with their non-alienative states (Fig. 4.1).

Blauner tried to measure the levels of alienation in different workplaces and suggests that this is primarily dependent on the dominant form of technology. He studied four types of industry, printing, textiles, car assembly and chemicals, which he saw as representative of four distinct types of technology, craft, machine-tending, assembly line and process technology. It is in the last case where computers have been used most extensively for production control. Capital-intensive plants that refine or process raw materials — chemicals, electricity, gas, food, petroleum, cement, paper etc. — are increasingly structured so that information on operations throughout the organization can be linked through computer-controlled networks. Sensors can measure and report details on flow rates of liquids, quality of materials, pressure on valves etc.

Dimensions of alienation	Non-alienative states
Powerlessness	Control
Meaninglessness	Purpose
Isolation	Social integration
Self-estrangement	Self-involvement

Figure 4.1   Blauner's dimensions of alienation

His findings led him to conclude that alienation was low on all four dimensions in the craft printing industry; high on three (with the exception of social isolation) in the case of machine-tending in textiles; and rose to its highest levels on the car assembly lines. However, he found in the process production of the chemical plants that alienation fell once more to the low levels of craft production, which produces his famous 'inverted U-curve' (Fig. 4.2). Workers were no longer tied for long hours to assembly lines where they carried out boring, repetitive tasks, but a small number of white-coated, trained technicians now used their expertise to check highly-automated plant. This enlarged their jobs and permitted them to apply their skills and knowledge in work that provided far higher levels of satisfaction.

Blauner's work has been criticized on many counts, but it has proved influential. The main implication of his thesis, as the title of his book *Alienation and Freedom* suggests, is that as technology advances — and thanks to micro-controlled robots our car factories come increasingly to resemble our chemical plants — so the drudgery of work is removed, alienation eliminated and workers freed to develop their skills. It suggests that mass-production assembly lines are best seen as a passing phase of history, and that

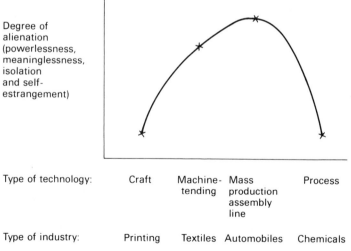

Figure 4.2 Blauner's 'inverted U-curve' relating alienation and technology

new technology affords the opportunity to return to high levels of job satisfaction found in earlier forms of craft work.

The optimists argue that microelectronics will provide a number of new, highly skilled jobs, mostly in the computer-related field. First, there will be a growing demand for engineering skills, particularly in the relating of microelectronics to control, production and mechanical systems. And secondly, there will be an increasing demand for logic, systems and software skills, and general data-processing awareness. During the early 1980s there was a shortage of such staff despite the growing levels of unemployment. A government study suggested there were 275 000 people with computer-related skills, but a further 25 000 were immediately needed. There was a shortage of 16 000 computer programmers and systems analysts, and a 6 per cent shortfall in electronics engineers in the computer supply industry.

APPLICATIONS OF NEW INFORMATION TECHNOLOGY

It is not difficult to see why the optimists are excited by new information technology: it can do amazing things. It can assist design, machining of parts, assembly, production control, quality control, stock control and maintenance. The range and variety of possible applications seems endless, and for convenience I shall adopt a series of headings and sub-headings to consider the major changes that might be expected in the factory situation.

Computer-aided design (CAD)

At the design stage of manufactured production, computers are increasingly used in areas such as production planning, engineering, architecture and even dress design. CAD can be used in two broad senses: first, to help design the production process within a manufacturing context and, second, to design the product itself. A factory production manager may use CAD to model the effect of a particular design on manufacturing schedules, while a skilled engineer might use it for creating a particular product. The computer's value as a design aid stems from its capacity to store, restructure and display vast amounts of information — on dimensions of components, raw materials, location of suppliers, unit costs of production, etc. — and it therefore doubles as both an electronic design board and a technical library.

Designers at computer-based work stations can devise, plan and even simulate the eventual design, size, cost, performance etc. of new products. This provides considerable advantages. In the first place, it removes much of the drudgery from the designer's work and allows the validity of various alternatives to be tested before a commitment to manufacture is made. From a technical point of view, it allows the product, building, dress or whatever to be viewed from a number of different angles. Three-dimensional models of houses, aircraft, power stations etc. can be created, allowing the designer to identify (and thereby rectify) any problem areas — such as stress factors — before the product is assembled. The architect, for instance, can experiment with variations in heating systems, wiring rings, window sizes, and calculate the cumulative effect they have. Perspectives can be changed swiftly with a light pen and features added and deleted. Trillions of bits of information can thus be stored in the databank and recalled, possibly years later, for safety checks or design changes. In 1981 there were only around 5000 CAD systems in the world, but now they are increasing at a rate of 50 per cent a year.

As in other areas, CAD will increasingly be affected by techno-logical convergence. A good example is the link that is developing with laser technology. Designers' scale models can now be 'filmed' whereby the surface of the model is subjected to light from a laser, which creates an image in thin air. This technology, termed holography, allows three-dimensional models of prospective pro-ducts to be used in sales presentations. Potential customers can walk round a building, bridge or car and view it from all sides, even though it only exists as an image.

Computer numerically controlled (CNC) machines and tools
Once the product is designed, it is then manufactured, and com-puter technology has played an important part in this stage of the production process ever since the emergence of computer numerically controlled (CNC) machines and tools in the early 1960s. In those days, numerically controlled machines were pro-grammed by punched paper tape, but this progressed to the use of more sophisticated computer control and what is today termed computer-aided manufacture (CAM). Such equipment is exten-sively used in milling, drilling and lathe work.

Machine tools were a prime target for automatic control because they work in a predetermined and repetitive fashion. A series of operations are programmed into the machine which can then perform the task endlessly without tiring. Various aspects of the machining process — cutting angle, speed, tool selection etc. — have therefore come under pre-programmed control, and any decisions are now made by the machine rather than the worker. Most engineering machine shop work is done in small runs of components and the coming of CNC machines and tools has provided far greater flexibility. They are still relatively expensive but, thanks to microelectronics, their cost is falling all the time, and their adoption becomes ever more widespread.

In some instances, CAM has been directly linked to the earlier CAD stage — to provide what engineers term computer-aided engineering (CAE) — as happens in electronics when integrated circuits are planned by CAD techniques and then sent direct by computers to the chip manufacturing stage. Under CAE, a single system can design components, display them graphically, produce design drawings, plan production schedules, prepare programs for machine tools, supervise production, maintain quality control and re-order parts. There are to date few instances of such systems in operation, but CAE is theoretically perfectly feasible.

Much of this, however, fades into insignificance when we consider the changes now on the horizon. Remarkable though CAM machines are, they are designed for particular functions, and though they can be re-programmed (e.g. to cut at a different angle) they cannot be switched between totally different tasks. It is when machines can be re-programmed for totally new operations that the factory obtains a flexibility it never had in the past. This moves us into the realm of robotics.

Robotics
The merging of microelectronics and mechanical engineering — what is commonly called megatronics — will have a substantial impact on manufacturing industry, and will most often take the form of robotic applications. The essential difference between a machine and a robot is that the former is purpose-built to perform a specific task while the robot's microprocessor–brain allows it to carry out a series of tasks, and can be re-programmed to amend or totally change those tasks. Once programmed, the robot can perform its tasks ad infinitum, and with far greater precision and

regularity than any human. Degrees of precision are now astonishing — with robots able to slot needles into minute holes — and this will continue to increase.

The advantages of robots are fivefold.

- Because of their greater consistency, the quality of production is enhanced. Robots do not tire, need tea-breaks, suffer boredom, sabotage machinery, fall ill or go on strike.
- In that robots can be re-programmed to perform different tasks, they offer far greater flexibility in production processes than traditional machinery.
- Robots can work in atmospheres hostile to human health, e.g. paint spray shops, coal mines, ocean beds etc. They have been introduced in many areas of dangerous, dirty work where absenteeism has traditionally been high.
- Output can be adjusted exactly to meet demand. At the Fiat car factories, robots are stopped if too many cars are being produced and apparently do not mind being 'laid off'!
- In the long term, robots can prove a considerable saving, particularly in terms of labour costs. Although the Fiat robotic line cost 30 per cent more than a conventional line, it now needs 25 workers instead of 125 to run it.

The industries most likely to be affected by robotics include metal and plastic fabrication, instrument engineering, electrical engineering, shipbuilding and marine engineering, vehicles, electronic components, office machinery, chemicals, printing, and aerospace. The American Society of Manufacturing Engineers at the University of Michigan predicts that by 1987, 15 per cent of all assembly systems in the United States will employ robot technology: by 1988, 50 per cent of labour in small-component assembly will be replaced by automation; and by 1990 the development of sensory techniques will enable robots to approximate human capability in assembly. Comparisons between robotized and non-robotized factories can be frightening in production terms. In 1980, British Leyland produced only 3.7 vehicles per employee per year compared with 69 at Toyota, Japan, and half as much overall as Volkswagen with a 20 per cent bigger workforce. Robotization now seems imperative for car manufacturers if they wish to remain competitive.

In medicine, robots will be able to carefully move bed-ridden patients and allow surgeons to perform operations by remote control from thousands of miles away. In fighting crime, there is now a robot that can make enquiries, temporarily blind a suspect with its spotlight, and call for help through its siren. In agriculture, robots are already being used to shear sheep, pluck chickens and (in Japan) classify fish. A leading Japanese university has a robot with human-type hands and legs, TV-camera eyes, artificial ears and mouth, and touch and joint sensing; it possesses some of the capabilities of a two- to three-year-old child.

The robot of science fiction has always resembled the human being, and though the industrial robots of today are somewhat different, at a simple level the analogy still holds. Robots consist of three main elements — the mechanical structure, the power unit and the control system — which we can interpret as the body, muscles and brain. Staying with the human analogy, the three key parts of a robot are the brain, the arm and the hand (or, as the technologists would term it, the 'grippers'). With rapid advancement in microelectronics, the first of these is now increasingly cheap, highly reliable, considerably sophisticated and capable of controlling a wide variety of tasks. The arm too, with advances in mechanical engineering, is increasingly versatile and dependable. It is the third area, the grippers, where robots are still weakest. Not surprisingly, therefore, robots have to date predominated in heavy engineering and been used in two main ways. First they have been used for various transfer operations such as moving metal components from one position to another, sorting or packing parts, and loading or unloading equipment. Robots can do all this most effectively, particularly where the workpiece may be heavy, hot or sharp. Secondly, robots have been used to undertake repetitive tasks with tools, particularly various forms of spraying, welding, cutting and grinding. This they can also do effectively, for once the tool is fixed in the robot's hand it requires no particular dexterity on the part of its fingers. Because the grippers remain the weak part of the robots' anatomy, they have to date not been used extensively in assembly (at least not in Britain) and certainly not outside the field of heavy engineering. But major changes are occurring: a second generation of 'intelligent' robots — mobile and multi-armed, able to 'see, hear, talk, and smell', and possessing a finer sense of touch — are now being developed (particularly in Japan) that will be able to perform most of the remaining tasks on the factory floor. The grippers — like the rest of the anatomy — will continue to improve, and industries like food, cosmetics and chemicals seem certain to be transformed.

Flexible manufacturing systems (FMS)

Convergence has been one of our recurring themes, and the next evolutionary stage from CNC machine tools, CAD, CAM and robotics is for all these various techniques to be linked through computerized communication and control systems, to form what is termed flexible manufacturing systems (FMS) which integrate all stages of the production process into a single automated operation.

As the title suggests, the great gains from FMS are increased flexibility (allowing small batches to be run without great difficulty) and more consistent quality of output. Because an FMS can be instantly re-programmed to make new parts or products, a single system can replace several different conventional machining lines, yielding huge savings in capital investment and plant size. Production machinery is inter-linked by automatic handling devices (such as robots), automatic transfer systems (such as guided pallets) and communication lines. The whole operation is supervised by a computer (or group of computers) which knows at any particular time where a specific workpiece is and what is happening to it. Mass production — so associated with the old style assembly line — now becomes replaced by batch production. This can be seen in the case of cars where, instead of standardized models, companies now use robots to build individual cars to customers' specifications with a variety of different accessories.

The production cycle is now keyed to the customer's order rather than manufacturing first and trying to sell the products later, greatly reducing the risk element from a manufacturer's point of view. In the past, batch manufacturing required machines designed to perform single tasks; and for each product change they had to be rebuilt or replaced. FMS brings a level of diversity never before obtainable, for different products can be made on the same line at will. Aircraft, tractors, office desks, large computers — all these products are now produced in batches rather than mass produced. All this makes it easier for the manufacturer to enter new markets and keep abreast of changes in fashion. Due to their cost, however, the number of systems (certainly in Britain) remains small.

Computerized stock control and warehousing

An important part of FMS is computerized stock control and warehousing. When a product is made, various parts and raw materials have to be delivered to the point of manufacture, while the completed products themselves have to be stored for distribution. It is estimated that at present up to 40 per cent of Britain's gross national product is spent on the storage and handling of goods produced in factories, and the economic gains from automation could be considerable. Automated fork-lift trucks, which can be programmed to go to particular parts of a warehouse, appeared in the late 1970s, and now Japan has over 2000 fully automated warehouses, compared to around 500 in West Germany and nearer 100 in Britain. If we could turn stock over as quickly as the West Germans, our levels could be reduced by 40 per cent, equivalent to releasing £20 billion of working capital. Japanese warehouses that once used twenty-five staff can now operate with four and the gains in speed, accuracy and access to information are considerable. At Volvo's plant in Koping, Sweden, stock inventories have been cut by 20 per cent, giving an annual saving in interest charges of over £100 000.

But investment in Britain seems likely to remain piecemeal, as the component parts of computerized warehousing — trucks, fork-lifts, cranes etc. — are made by different companies and we do not think in terms of integrating them together in systems as others appear to do. British Leyland are one major company who have been adventurous in this field: the vast automated parts store at the Longbridge West works is run by seven minicomputers which record and check the quality and quantity of all parts. When needed, the items in stock are not retrieved by hand, but by robots. The parts store itself is linked up to every other section of the factory through 4½ miles of video data cable. This provides a continuous flow of information on stock levels, quality control and production levels. Managers anywhere in the plant can tap into the system through visual display units (VDUs) to see how other sections are operating. Needless to say, the whole system was designed by a computer.

Towards the automated factory

The impetus towards technological convergence seems unstoppable, and just as electronics, telecommunications and computing converged to form information technology, so CNC tools, robots and automated materials handling are converging to form flexible manufacturing systems and, ultimately, the automated factory. Eventually the whole system could work like this. In response to an order, computerized plans would be produced from the factory's design office; instructions would go to the warehouse for certain raw materials; and these would be taken to the point of production by automated fork-lift trucks and robots. The parts would be machined by CNC machine tools controlled by robots and, when machining is completed, robots would carry out the tasks of assembling, welding, painting and quality control. Volvo of Sweden have calculated that such a factory could be designed with existing technology to produce 1200 vehicles a day using a workforce of twelve. So we move towards the factory that just has one man and a dog: the dog is there to make sure no one touches the machinery, and the man is there to feed the dog!

The most celebrated FMS example is the Fanuc plant just outside Tokyo where robots controlled by computers make other robots. Fanuc (a subsidiary of the giant Fujitsu group) makes 100 robots a month with the minimum of human intervention, and during the night shift, one man does the work that previously occupied 200. Fanuc estimate that it would have needed ten times the capital investment for the same output with conventional technology; it would also have needed about ten times the labour force of around 100. All in all, the plant is about five times as productive as a conventional factory. In terms of FMS, Japan is way ahead of any other nation. While the whole of United States industry can boast just over thirty systems, one major Japanese company alone, Toyoda Machine Tool Co., has the same number. But automated factories are beginning to emerge in the United States, as they are in Bulgaria, the Soviet Union and certain European countries, including Britain.

Britain's first unmanned factory opened in Colchester, Essex, in 1982, as a government-sponsored showpiece, though it does operate as a standard factory. It is a £3 million small batch production line making a variety of shafts, gears and discs in steel, cast iron and aluminium. The raw component is loaded automatically on to a pallet and carried on a conveyor belt past various machine tools (drilling, cutting, chamfering etc.). The robot picks up the component and presents it to the appropriate machine tool for machining. After this, the robot releases the component and passes it along the conveyor for the next machining operation, while sensor devices monitor progress and a technician checks the VDUs. When one batch of components is finished, the technician resets the program for the next batch (Fig. 4.3).

The factory can produce finished components in a three-day cycle, whereas the former manual operations took ten to twelve weeks' work and involved fifty separate handlings of the different small batches of orders. As we noted earlier, the advantages from such a factory lie not so much in labour-saving as in its adaptability — reducing stocks and manufacturing time-cycles, overcoming unsocial working hours, quickly reacting to market changes etc. The only people employed in the factory are a handful of white-collar operators to switch on and check operations.

Automated plants are now becoming more common in Britain. Rolls Royce have turned a Derby tram shed into an automated plant to make turbine blades for the engines of the Boeing 757. Blades can now be made in 45 seconds instead of 6 minutes, and six men are employed instead of thirty. Inventory costs have been halved and productivity has been increased by 28 per cent per employee.

In Somerset, Normalair-Garrett have built a £1 million auto-mated plant for the production of bomb-release mechanisms. The

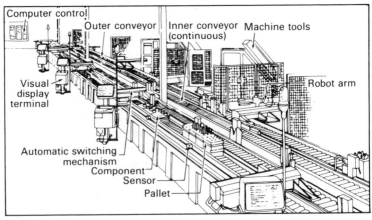

Figure 4.3   The automated factory

(*Source*: Zorkoczy, 1985)

manufacturing cycle time is down from four months to two weeks; stock is turned over six times faster; only two to three operators work on each shift; and output per employee has increased from £67 000 per year to £210 000.

A key aim of the GEC robotic project is to produce a £25 million prototype automated factory. This will include all the interlocking techniques of automated production — second-generation robots, computer run machine tools linked directly to product-design computers, high-power lasers, and automated warehouses run by computer-controlled driverless trucks.

Computer-integrated manufacture (CIM)

The ultimate convergence is for the unmanned factory to be automatically linked with the electronic office and other information systems within the work organization, in a process labelled computer-integrated manufacture (CIM). CAM, CAD, monitoring and testing, automated materials handling — all are combined with management planning, production planning and control functions to form a total system. A computer — complete with database and data network — optimizes production flow and scheduling to meet the production plan, and all operations are interlinked so that production is tightly controlled at every stage. The technology for CIM is already with us but at present most British firms are nowhere near implementing such systems.

THE DESKILLING ARGUMENT

The immediate impression is that there is much here to be welcomed. I for one would be quite happy to see robots go into paint spray shops and get their lungs filled with poisonous fumes rather than workers; I wouldn't mind if robots lost their fingers on machines rather than operatives; and I would welcome the release of humans from tedious assembly-line tasks. Robots could help us automate out of existence some of the most boring, repetitive, noisy, dirty, unhealthy and dangerous jobs in industrial society. If, in addition, the work that remains can be made more skilled and responsible, then this seems all to the good, and one can see why many welcome new technology as liberating and beneficial.

Why, then, are others sceptical? In the first place, as we saw in the last chapter, there is fear over job loss. Even if new jobs are created, they seem unlikely to be in manufacturing companies employing robots. The whole point of robots is that they are designed to replace humans, and though they did not arouse initial hostility — when they were used to undertake unpalatable work like paint spraying — resistance can be expected when they spread further in manufacturing industry. In Japan — where there was little concern over unemployment up to 1982 — Nissan has signed an agreement with its house union (the first of its kind) guaranteeing that workers will not be demoted, or suffer wages cuts or worse employment conditions as a result of robotic installations. Management is now required to provide proper retraining before putting workers on new jobs and must consult with the trade union over any plans for installations.

In West Germany, a study by the Commerzbank in 1983 concluded that around half of the 1.2 million assembly-line jobs in West Germany would be threatened by the second-generation 'intelligent' robots before the 1990s. They argued that every robot installed today replaces three workers on average, and with the new robots the figure could rise to between five and ten. From five to seven thousand semi-skilled workers lost their jobs to robots between 1972 and 1982, and 90 per cent of all spot-welding and paint spraying could be robotized by 1990. Volkswagen have calculated that second-generation robots will do 60 per cent of all work in the car industry, and an OECD report estimates that by 1987 robots will have claimed 15 per cent of all US assembly jobs. In Britain, the effects to date have not been great due to the relatively slower take-up, but they can be expected to intensify.

As to more qualitative issues — the main concern of this chapter — the pessimists are equally despondent that the tasks people will be offered will become less skilled and rewarding. Braverman questions the suggestion that increased mechanization somehow raises skill levels, because the discussion is always couched in general terms, and talk of 'averages' ignores specific work situations. While we might accept that 'on average' skills have risen as a result of technological advancement, Braverman maintains that this ignores the widening chasm between those with very high technical skills and those in increasingly unskilled work. He graphically suggests that to talk in averages is like a man with one foot in ice and the other in fire saying that 'on average' he is perfectly comfortable!

He also questions the way optimists define 'skill' and interpret statistics on changing work patterns. As labourers declined and machine operatives increased, so the latter came to be labelled 'semi-skilled', but Braverman questions the case for doing this. Why is the labourer judged to be of lower skill than the operative? In that mechanization inevitably led to an increase in the operative ranks, this was bound to give support to the reskilling argument. Similarly in the 1950s a further category of 'service' workers was added to the census statistics, and as 25 per cent came from the 'semi-skilled' and 75 per cent from the 'unskilled', this again provided another instant upgrading. However, it is questionable whether the growing ranks of white-collar workers — who are invariably placed higher than manual workers in terms of occupational grading — exhibit higher levels of skill.

As to the suggestion that an increase in skilled work is reflected in the growing importance of universal education, Braverman replies that literacy and numeracy are essential requirements for modern *society*, but not necessarily modern occupations. Some jobs may demand high levels of training, and the education system acts as a filtering device to identify this elite, but this does not mean that *all* the population need more education. For Braverman, the link between education and work is tenuous, and most school-leavers are grossly over-educated for the work we offer them to do.

But the pessimists not only reject the reskilling argument. They believe there are clear signs that new information technology will intensify the historical tendency for all work to be continually deskilled under capitalism. These fears can be considered with reference to the design and production process; health and safety factors; and work monitoring and pacing.

The design process

New technology could dramatically affect the factory in terms of its layout, organization and scheduling. Major technology companies and top management can install systems which substantially alter and re-arrange people's work — in terms of skills, supervision, work shifts etc. — and the deskilling writers insist that workers and trade unions should be fully involved in any installations. The Conference of Socialist Economists (CSE) writers (1980) stress that system design is first and foremost a political and organizational activity rather than a merely technical one, and therefore consultation should take place at all stages and be formalized in new technology agreements.

Similar fears are expressed in connection with the design of the product and the adoption of CAD. While the computer can be used to carry out the routine or non-creative parts of the designer's job — drawing, listing parts, specification of techniques etc. — and provide new techniques and facilities which the worker decides how and when to use, it can also deskill highly trained architects and engineers by forcing them to operate within fixed constraints. The architect may no longer be free to draw on his imagination, but instead has to work with blocks of prescribed shape and length — rather like a child building with a Lego set — predetermined by the computer software. The outcome is that buildings grow depressingly alike — boring concrete blocks composed of standard parts — as the modern architect becomes incapable of ever conceiving a York Minster or Brighton Pavilion. The same points can be made with regard to engineering and dress design: the creative abilities of the designer become restricted by the dictates of the software.

The production process

As regards the production process, the CSE writers acknowledge that microelectronics offers the potential to re-humanize jobs but they see little likelihood of this happening. In their view it will not be introduced to meet human needs but rather to boost private profit, and any benefits will be incidental.

The introduction of CNC tools is quoted as an early example of computer technology deskilling highly trained workers. Machinists in small batch production traditionally held high status as skilled workers who had gained considerable experience through a long period of training. Tasks included assisting with production planning, setting up the machine, and controlling its speed and operation. The worker had to confer with both the designer and management, and yet retained considerable independence in his own work. Now, pessimists claim, he has less opportunity for contact with others and experiences a sense of isolation in his work situation.

With CNC machine tools, the skills of the machinist are broken down into their component parts and the computer programmed to control the operation of the machine tool. Control of the tool is thus transferred from the operator to the systems specialist, who analyses his skills. The machinist's job is now one of monitoring the computer-controlled equipment, a job that might be eliminated altogether once robots have been trained to do it or CNC systems become totally reliable.

The pessimists maintain that while new technology may in theory make possible the fully automated workplace, it will not be introduced by employers unless it is judged economically viable. Britain is still a low-wage economy relative to most advanced industrialized nations and, particularly in times of high unemployment, employers will use unskilled workers rather than invest in robotic equipment if it is cheaper to do so. This has the added advantage that they are seen as providing employment rather than automating people out of work with new technology. Britain's modest robotic development has therefore largely been as a *response* to the unemployment situation, not the *cause* of it. What seems more likely is that managers will introduce robots for highly skilled, intricate, heavy, delicate tasks (and save themselves the costs of skilled workers' wages) but retain unskilled workers (on low wages) in the more mundane, repetitive tasks. This could mean production lines composed of workers and robots in conjunction, in which the workers have to work at the pace of the impersonal, tireless robots. The CSE writers insist that companies should install telechrics (high technology systems that are completely controlled by the workers) rather than robotics, and where workers and robots work together, it is crucial that workers control the speed of work.

Health and safety
Health and safety have become major topics of concern, particularly in connection with the effects of VDUs. This will be discussed more in the next chapter on the office, but some factory workers may spend considerable time at terminals, and other forms of new technology may also involve hazards.

Cooley (1984) maintains there is a fundamental contradiction in the human/machine interface.

> The human being is the dialectical opposite of the machine in that he or she is slow, inconsistent, unreliable but highly creative. The machine on the other hand may be regarded as fast, consistent, reliable but totally non-creative.

The optimists may present these characteristics as complementary and supportive, but Cooley argues that as the computer dramatically increases the rate at which material is handled, so the stress on the worker trying to make qualitative judgements intensifies. He quotes American research which shows that those working with computers in the field of engineering design can experience creativity decreases of 30 to 40 per cent in the first hour and 80 per cent in the second.

While new technology may therefore reduce (or even remove) the strain of many tasks, their replacement with jobs that require the monitoring of dials and taking occasional action can create strains of a new kind. The problems of physical fatigue may merely be replaced by those of perceptual fatigue. The machinery may require rapid responses from operating staff to avoid dangerous developments, and this can create considerable stress. Nor is concentration helped by the fact that the product they are working on could now be far less visible. Finally, the introduction of new technology may be accompanied by new patterns of shiftwork so that maximum use can be obtained from expensive equipment. In 1954, only one in eight were shiftworkers, but this had risen to one in five by 1964 and is now around one in three. Some studies in West Germany claim that ulcers are eight times more common among shiftworkers; the divorce rate is 80 per cent higher; and juvenile delinquency among children of shiftworkers 50 per cent greater.

The last two decades have witnessed substantial increases in absence from work, not just due to physical illness, but more especially psychological illnesses (e.g. neurosis, nervous breakdowns, ulcers, headaches, blood pressure etc.), particularly among women. Seventy times as many working days are lost in Britain through sickness, and twice as many through accidents, as through strikes, and this could intensify further with new technology. Workers can experience stress if there are extremes (in either direction) of heat, noise, light, workload, responsibility, human contact etc. A satisfactory work situation requires a delicate balance between these factors, and consideration should be given to them in introducing new technology. Warr and Wall (1975) identify the following jobs as being particularly prone to stress:

● Repetitive, fast, strenuous production line work (e.g. manufacturing workers).

- Tense, responsible, concentrated work (e.g. air traffic controllers, surgeons, miners etc.).
- Work which involves conflicting demands from those above and below (e.g. foremen).

All these areas of work could well be significantly affected by new technology and produce increased stress factors.

Work monitoring and pacing

A lot of new technology applications have built in sub-systems for worker monitoring and pacing which allow management to check the quality and speed of work at any time. Such devices enable management to (a) measure workers' performance, (b) ensure the way a task is carried out, (c) collate information on employees, and (d) influence promotion prospects and career paths.

The autonomy of those who work with CNC machine tools, for instance, is reduced by monitoring systems which check daily output at a central control point and print out the exact output for each machine, and by systems that register at a control console if a worker is away from his position for more than the prescribed time. Advertisements for word processors often stress the fact that managers can easily determine the number of words inputted per minute and the number of mistakes made. The tachograph — 'the spy in the cab' which is now compulsory under EEC regulations for long-distance lorries — records a vehicle's speed at every stage of the journey, and any stops made. PBX telephone exchanges can print out all calls made, the extensions they come from, and their destination, duration and cost. Supermarket check-out machines have similar devices, and these can be expected to spread to other work situations. The CSE writers maintain that although the technology itself may be neutral, the functioning system is not and is usually designed in oppressive ways. Though such devices may be justified by employers in terms of greater efficiency and management effectiveness, the pessimists view them as mechanisms for extending management control and an unwarranted intrusion into individuals' work situations. To them it is the further spread of Taylorism into areas of intellectual work: it reduces independence, trust and responsibility, and is another stage in the deskilling process.

Alternative design

The CSE writers argue that to counter these dangers, workers must insist on certain safeguards and companies think in terms of 'alternative design'. They make the following demands:

● New technology should involve higher pay and no loss of jobs.
● Workers should retain some control over the design process, and any changes to factory layout and working arrangements only be made in accordance with new technology agreements.
● Checks should constantly be made on health and safety factors in line with the 1974 Act.
● Companies should be encouraged to install telechrics rather than robotics. Where workers and robots work together, workers should control the speed of work.
● Built-in sub-systems for worker monitoring and pacing should be designed out.

CRITIQUE OF THE DESKILLING ARGUMENT

Optimists level two main criticisms at those who advocate the deskilling argument. First they accuse them of adopting a short-term perspective (e.g. twenty years) and highlighting possible difficulties in the transitional period while ignoring long-term benefits. Though in the short run, new technology may create some job displacement, deskilling or work alongside robots, in the long term it should allow fully automated production and the utopian society Marx always envisaged, without violent revolution. In short, this is similar to the long-term optimistic view of the previous chapter. The deskilling writers are accused of complaining about the nature of most modern work, but then moaning when new information technology arrives to overcome so many of the problems they are concerned about. Capitalists have shown themselves adaptable in the past, allowing workers to improve their rights of citizenship and material conditions; why should this not happen again?

The second major criticism of the deskilling writers is that they tend to underplay the intrinsic characteristics of different technologies and their vast range of possible applications. Because new technology is rather viewed *as a whole* (i.e. as a tool of the ruling class), the fact that it can produce varying effects in different work sectors is somewhat ignored. Rosenbrock *et al.* (1981), however, argue that the *pace* of change could vary markedly from one sector to another and present their arguments under three broad headings.

(a)   Process production
In process industries (oil, chemicals, glass, paper, cement, iron and steel making etc.) continuous production methods have been in operation for some time and microelectronics seems unlikely to have any marked effect as levels of automation are already high. In such plants, microcomputers could well be used as an alternative to single, central, mainframe systems (i.e. new technology will be used to improve what is already done). There will probably be greater integration of operations through automatic data gathering, and in the long term some new processes might become feasible (e.g. through biotechnology). The labour force is already small so further reductions are not a serious economic consideration and, for safety reasons, this may not be possible anyway. The nature of the work should not greatly change, though it is matter of debate whether it is presently highly skilled.

(b)   Engineering production
In this field, CNC tools and machines, and robots, are spreading, and CAD/CAM offers considerable scope for development. Certain workers in design sections and on assembly lines may well be replaced by technological advances, and those remaining may find aspects of their work deskilled.

(c)   Office work
Office work — correspondence, ordering, invoicing etc. — has traditionally been labour-intensive, and this will substantially change, both in quantitative and qualitative terms, with the coming of new information technology. With word processors, viewdata, electronic mail etc., considerable labour displacement can be expected, with the nature of the jobs for those remaining significantly changing.

The effects, therefore, could well be uneven, with change occurring more rapidly in, say, a car factory than a chemical plant. These arguments can be summarized as in Table 4.1.

Leaving aside the office — which is our concern in the next chapter — this has a similar ring to Blauner and perhaps brings us full circle. The key point is that the optimists strongly emphasize the

Table 4.1   The likely effects of new information technology on different industrial sectors

	Process	*Engineering*	*Office*
Labour displacement	Low	Moderate	High
Technological investment	Moderate	Increasing	High
Time-scale	Long term	Intermediate	Immediate

difference between manufacturing and process production, arguing that the latter provides more highly skilled work, and that as automation gathers pace and manufacturing plants turn to continuous flow production, so the deskilling aspects of factory work will evaporate. The pessimists, on the other hand, do not expect the production line to disappear overnight, and even when and if it does, they question whether process production in a capitalist society necessarily provides fulfilling, non-alienating work.

Personally, I find Rosenbrock's distinctions useful, and would actually take them a stage further. Recent research (see Piercy *et al.*) suggests we can expect considerable variation, not only between different areas of work, but even between different companies in the *same* sectors. Some companies, for instance, train their machinists to program CNC machine tools which can help provide a wider range of techniques for the skilled worker. Much also depends on national policies. In Sweden, for example, workers are automatically involved in all aspects of plant and system design, and at Volvo have a say in determining the size of work groups and whether robots are included. This reaffirms the point that it is dangerous to adopt a wholly optimistic or pessimist view; it greatly comes down to choice.

CHAPTER FIVE

The Office

If one regards most factory work as already severely deskilled, then the threat of new technology is to some extent muted. If work conditions are already so dreadful, is there that much to lose? If the pace of the line, the surveillance of the manager and the noise of the machinery are already so intense that one is unable to communicate with fellow workers, is working alongside robots that much worse? The removal of some tasks altogether (and certainly the possible creation of new skills) might even be worth the price of deskilling others. The impact of the technology is therefore relative to the existing situation. This, in part, explains why many commentators maintain that changes in the factory will not be as marked as those in the office.

There are two distinct phases to the so-called office revolution. As of now, technology is mainly being used to assist the efficiency of operations already being carried out (i.e. the word processor replaces the typewriter, the microcomputer replaces the filing cabinet etc.). The second phase — brought about by the convergence of electronic data processing, telecommunications and office machines — involves the total elimination of many intermediary functions, and affects the workings of not just the individual office, but the whole work enterprise. We can distinguish between 'information workers' — involved in the routine entry, recording, storage and transmission of information — and 'knowledge workers', who analyse and utilize it. Phase one will affect the first group, which includes typists, clerks and data entry personnel, while phase two will also include the knowledge workers. The first phase is the central concern of this chapter, while the second phase is considered in the next.

It is generally accepted that new technology will transform the office more than anywhere else. We saw in Chapter 3 that there is widespread agreement that it will lead to considerable displacement, and similar fears are expressed over deskilling. But it goes further than this. Office work has traditionally been regarded as congenial, respectable, clean, flexible, quiet and non-authoritarian, and some fear that these characteristics too will be destroyed. It is historically a form of work that carries higher status — partly because of the greater opportunity to mix with management — and this could also be lost. In particular, it has long provided an attractive source of employment for women — 70 per cent of clerical workers and 99 per cent of secretaries are women — and new information technology could adversely affect their job opportunities.

It is not just that the nature of work could change for the worse, but the whole working environment. Consequently the terms reskilling and deskilling tend to be somewhat narrow for our purposes and I usually revert to the broader optimistic and pessimistic labels. I shall draw in particular on the work of Vincent Guiliano (1982) and Hazel Downing (1980), and — because of the vast variety of clerical occupations — focus principally on secretarial work, which is being significantly affected by what is probably the most widespread form of office automation — word processing (WP).

Why is it expected that change in the office will be even greater than in the factory? In the first place, while new technology for production processes is often purpose-made, most office equipment can be mass produced which should encourage ease of application and further cost reductions. But more important, the office has long been labour-intensive and under-capitalized in comparison with manufacturing industry. Office workers have come to form an increasing part of the workforce — 45 per cent by 1980 — but only £500 of capital stock is invested for the average office worker compared with £5000 for each shopfloor worker. Direct office costs in the United States were estimated at a million million dollars in 1982, but while 75 per cent of this went on salaries, only 7 per cent went on information-handling resources. The effect of this has been that the increase in white-collar employment has not been matched in terms of increased productivity. It has been estimated in America that, over the past ten years, while productivity has increased 200 per cent for farmers and 100 per cent for factory workers, it has gone up for office workers by just 4 per cent.

The cheaper electronic systems now offer the opportunity to redress this balance. During the 1970s, while office salaries continued to rise each year, costs for communication equipment, computer logic and computer memory came *down* at annual rates of 11, 25 and 40 per cent respectively. It has been estimated that there are around 20 million million A4 pages stored in American offices, and this is growing by a million pages every minute. Apart from the problem of physical storage, this also creates the organizational difficulty of locating particular documents when needed. Office workers are estimated to spend around a quarter of their time looking for information. New information technology therefore offers gains in terms of productivity storage and retrieval, and is an area ripe for investment.

Employers have been attracted by these opportunities. By 1982 there were 100 000 micro-based systems at work in British offices compared with 40 000 in 1980 and barely a handful prior to 1978. In the United States (where the use of office technology has been most widespread), some 38 million terminal-based work stations can be expected in offices, factories and schools by 1990, and there could be 34 million home terminals and 7 million portable terminals. Word processing in particular is booming, growing by over 30 per cent a year, and worth around £4 billion worldwide in 1985.

OFFICE ORGANIZATION

Guiliano suggests that office organization has gone through three main stages of development, each involving major changes, particularly in the sphere of technological innovation.

The pre-industrial office

This emerged in the latter half of the nineteenth century and was characterized by low levels of mechanization and close personal relations. The 'counting house' — which contained the three principal characters of boss, clerk and boy — was personal, small and involved little division of labour. In this Dickensian style office, the clerk — who was almost certainly male, middle class and educated — would work for the boss very much as a personal assistant, and probably hoped one day to become a private businessman himself. Even if his wages were humble, he was of a different status to the artisans because he possessed basic numeracy and literacy and was able to fraternize with the business class. Operations largely depended on the performance of individuals without much recourse to either systematic work organization or mechanization. Little conscious attention was paid to work flow efficiency or productivity of methods.

This form of office still exists today in many small business, general management and executive offices; good human relations (loyalty, trust, respect etc.) are the key features and any information-handling devices (telephones, copiers, word processors etc.), while useful, are not utilized to maximum advantage. This structure is generally only effective so long as operations remain small-scale, and becomes inefficient for handling large volumes of transactions or complex procedures requiring the co-ordination of different data sources.

Over time, the pre-industrial office faded in most organizations. We witnessed a growth in the number of clerks (from 0.8 per cent of workers in 1851 to 10 per cent by 1951); an increase in the number of female clerks (from 0.1 per cent in 1851 to 59.6 per cent by 1951); the growth of larger offices; the growth of an 'under class' intake due to universal education; and the increasing use of mechanization. Thus we moved from the 'pre-industrial' to the 'industrial' office.

The industrial office
By the turn of the century, significant technological change had taken place. Steel nibs came to replace quill pens, and typewriters were being manufactured. This was followed by electric type-writers, telephone switchboards, ticker tape, photocopying machines, adding machines, calculators, dictating machines, data-processing equipment etc., and created the industrial office we know today. But as with the factory, it was not the technology itself so much as the workplace restructuring it implied that was so significant. Just as the principles of Taylorism entered the factory, so they now entered the office, and workers became subjected to work study.

In the large, impersonal, industrial office, workers are organized to serve the needs of a production system. Work becomes simplified, specialized and regulated, with the result that jobs are often boring, repetitive and unsatisfying as the office becomes a 'production line' with paper moving horizontally between desks as each clerk performs a particular stage. To sustain this paper flow, workers must now work fixed hours, and the office becomes subject to the rigid work patterns of the factory. This approach has proved particularly suitable for offices handling large volumes of customer transactions (e.g. insurance companies), and using batch systems for mainframe computers, for this demands standardization of jobs, transactions, technologies and even personal interactions. Thus in the industrial office much work becomes deskilled and akin to factory production.

Guiliano concedes that the industrial office has a number of shortcomings. From a human point of view, many find the work tedious and this can become apparent to customers and managers with whom they often have to deal. If anything, clerical workers can become *more* alienated than their factory counterparts as they have to constantly give the impression that they actually enjoy their jobs. From a technical point of view, the industrial office is also criticized because many errors arise from the human-operated production process, and — because of the sub-division of tasks — these often become compounded rather than rectified. Finally, from the employer's point of view, office work is highly labour-intensive, and thereby costly.

The information office
We are now entering a further period of transition as data processing and telecommunications technology converge to form what has variously been described as the information, paperless or electronic office. The object is to merge techniques of computer processing, storage of data, retrieval of data and data communications to improve efficiency. In future, the typewriter, telephone, facsimile machine, printer and computer will all use the same digital language based on the binary code. Terminal-based work stations will be linked with a continuously updated data base to provide integrated systems capable of handling electronically almost every office function. The key developments are large capacity, cheap computer storage, word processing equipment and cheap, reliable telecommunications equipment. This will create a world in which managers, at the touch of a button, send memos to each other 10 000 miles apart; instantly obtain data for meetings from their company's electronic files; employ electronic calendars to schedule meetings at times when all colleagues are free; and chat simul-

taneously with colleagues around the world in teleconferences. Paper ceases to be needed, as everything is done electronically, and we move from the industrial to the information office.

NEW OFFICE TECHNOLOGY

We can consider office activities under three main headings, and each area could be profoundly affected by new information technology.

The written word

The piece of technology most associated with document preparation is the typewriter which has evolved through its various stages — mechanical, electric, electronic — to the word processor. The key change is that data is now processed according to a standard digital character code, which makes it compatible with computers, and allows for the storage and manipulation of text and graphics before it is reconverted to printed form. This will lead on to the development of optical character recognition (OCR) equipment which can 'read' people's handwriting and convert it into digital form. Eventually, as we noted in Chapter 1, we can expect machines that will convert from the human voice.

This technological convergence assists companies with the considerable problem of inter-organizational communication. Buildings can now be cabled to form local area networks (LANs) so that different sorts of terminals can be hooked together and data sent at high speed to various destinations. Just as one can plug different electrical appliances into various sockets on a wiring circuit in one's home, so data can be circulated to terminals at all points of the organization. A message originating on a word processor may travel to a central computer and on to a mini or microcomputer in another part of the building. Once installed, this can substitute the flow of computer-coded information for the flow of paper, and even provide links with other national and international data networks. In such a situation we can expect 'multifunction work stations' in which the desk, telephone, typewriter and filing cabinet are replaced by a single electronic box. In terms of distribution, the established methods of telex and facsimile transmission will give way to a computerized teletex network which will provide a far superior and swifter service. With satellites, several hundred pages can be transmitted every minute compared with one A4 page every 3 minutes with traditional methods.

To summarize, a communication, such as a personal letter, would now go through the following stages. It would be typed on a keyboard, displayed on a VDU and sent through the telecommunications system in digital form. At the other end it would join a 'queue' of communications where it could be read on the recipient's VDU. The recipient can then call up all communications, and destroy, store or print them.

The spoken word

If the key technology for transmission of the written word has been the typewriter, for the spoken word it is the telephone. This will remain the key technology, but again will become increasingly versatile, fast, cheap and reliable through technological advances. Dictating and automatic answering machines are already widely used, but these will now be joined by multi-connection for telephone conferencing; abbreviated dialling for long, regularly-used numbers; repeat dialling, when lines are engaged; diverting facilities, whereby all incoming calls can be switched to a specified number; and automatic reminder calls.

Management aids

The principal aim of any office is not to produce more information, or to produce it more quickly, but to make more effective use of it, and computer aids can help in this process by making information more manageable.

Computerized information systems within industrial organizations can be considered at three hierarchical levels, and each stage has developed as technological sophistication has increased. The first systems were introduced for 'number crunching' activities such as payroll. These systems are 'pre-specified' in that their processing functions are determined in advance and usually cannot be changed by the end user. They perform the role of collecting and processing the daily transactions of business and provide information not only for the organization, but customers, shareholders, government etc. Office support systems are more 'personalized' and enable management and office personnel to

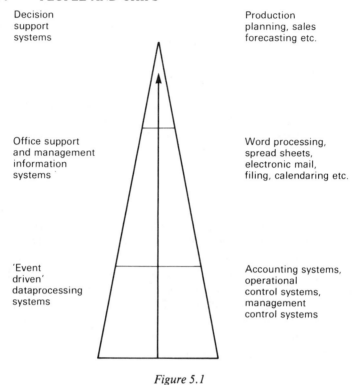

Decision
support
systems

Production
planning, sales
forecasting etc.

Office support
and management
information
systems

Word processing,
spread sheets,
electronic mail,
filing, calendaring etc.

'Event
driven'
dataprocessing
systems

Accounting systems,
operational
control systems,
management
control systems

Figure 5.1

process and obtain information swiftly and efficiently. For the middle manager, packages such as financial planning spreadsheets allow for superior data collection and analysis, and should assist decision-making.

The most sophisticated systems are decision support systems which enable managers to simulate particular situations to assess the possible effects of particular strategies. Underlying trends can be fed into a system as hypothetical courses of action are considered, and some systems even provide recommendations for management. Such systems are expensive, not yet widely used and mainly confined to top managers of large companies. All three systems overlap in the sense that one develops from another; all operate concurrently; and decision support systems rely on the data-processing systems as a source for much of their data.

THE OPTIMISTIC VIEWPOINT

Optimists, such as Guiliano, argue that the information age office has the potential for combining systems and machines to the mutual benefit of both workers and clients. They see it as preserving the best aspects of earlier stages while avoiding their failings. Workers now experience a greater variety of work, for they control all information added to the master data base, are responsible for making any corrections, and come to handle a wider range of transactions. Much repetitive work (e.g. retyping, manual filing and retrieving etc.) is now eliminated. Productivity ceases to be measured in quantitative terms by the number of hours worked or items processed, but by the quality of the service the customer receives. Though Guiliano acknowledges that labour displacement may be as high as 50 per cent, he optimistically concludes that those employees who remain benefit from a marked improvement in the quality of their working life.

A similarly optimistic line is presented in much of the management literature emanating on the office.

There is a trend away from being a small cog in a large wheel. People no longer want to perform repetitively a small part of an overall job. They want to have the satisfaction of doing an *entire* job well ... In the past, a purchase order or invoice had to be handled by many people because of the limitations of a paper-based system. With current technology individuals now can be responsible for an entire job since all the information they need can be provided at their fingertips. Not only is the efficiency of the workplace improved, but morale also can be raised, further increasing potential productivity. (Arthur Andersen and Co., 1985)

Optimists see considerable gains in terms of administrative effectiveness. 'Information float' — where delay and confusion are often caused by the unavailability of material that is being typed, in the mail, missing etc. — is greatly reduced, and accessibility and retrieval vastly improved. Management can make use of electronic mail, calendars, filing, all of which makes for swifter and better decisions. A further advantage is that cost reductions should prove considerable: electronic mail is only one-tenth the cost of conventional mail, and electronic filing is cheaper in that it saves a great deal of space.

New information technology also provides far greater flexibility. There is no longer any need to assemble all workers at the same time and place, for portable terminals and computers allow an 'office' to exist wherever the worker happens to be. Processing can now be done at a distance, as for instance when a manager dictates a letter at home and transmits it automatically down the line so that it appears on a machine in his office (or perhaps his secretary's home). The secretary can then prepare the documentation and transmit it in digital form to anywhere on the globe.

This permits greater mobility and flexibility in work arrangements, and is of particular benefit to the housebound, handicapped or those with domestic commitments. Guiliano illustrates this well by suggesting that the effects of microelectronics are analogous to those of the telephone. Because of its almost universal distribution, the worker does not have to 'go to work' to make a phone call, but they still have to do so to open mail, dictate a letter, read a file etc. This will now change as electronic mail, teleconferencing, working from home etc. become commonplace and create flexible new work patterns and rejuvenate the office to the benefit of all.

This is not to say that industrial-style offices will disappear overnight for people are used to the structure of an office schedule, and early research suggests that working from home and teleconferencing are not always that popular. The office will also continue to house centralized forms of communications technology too expensive for the home, and we might therefore enter a transitional period in which workers still go to the office — but not as frequently as they used to — before it finally fades away as new patterns, possibilities and preferences emerge.

THE PESSIMISTIC VIEWPOINT

The contrasting pessimistic viewpoint is seen in the work of Downing which, while concentrating on the secretary rather than clerical workers in general, argues that office work will become increasingly deskilled. The secretary emerged as a specialist office worker with the growth of record-keeping in industrial production and the increased utilization of typewriters, but the pessimists' fear is that with the arrival of new information technology (and especially word processors) secretarial work will be hit detrimentally in four main respects: employment, health and safety, job satisfaction, and social relations.

Employment

As regards employment, we saw in Chapter 3 that it is widely agreed that new technology will reduce employment levels in the office sector. The rate at which this will occur is largely unknown, for the signs are that firms will not adopt word processors overnight (particularly in time of recession) and they only provide marked gains for about a third of typing jobs. Nor do we know whether firms will use new technology to expand their quality and range of services or just to cut staff. But the studies quoted earlier show the effects can be dramatic. That new technology can cause labour displacement in a highly labour-intensive area like the office is not seriously challenged — particularly in phase two of the office revolution — and Guiliano would of course agree with Downing on this point.

Health and safety

An area of equal concern — largely held over from the last chapter — is that of health and safety, particularly as it relates to possible ill-effects from working long periods at VDUs. Early research indicated the possibility of hazardous effects on the eyes, causing fatigue, irritation and tension, and it was also alleged that they caused backache and emitted possibly dangerous levels of radiation. Tests in France and the United States showed an increase in short-sightedness, and a major fear was that pregnant women could be affected, a higher number of miscarriages being found in some instances compared with the general population.

The evidence for this, however, is far from conclusive. A report from the Health and Safety Executive, 1983, concluded that VDUs do *not* give out dangerously high levels of radiation, and pregnant women should not be adversely affected, though there may be a slight risk for people susceptible to cataracts and photo-sensitive epilepsy. Any other soreness, headaches etc. they suggest are more likely due to lighting and other ergonomic factors. This is confirmed by other research which supports the view that it is probably not the technology itself that causes stress, so much as the way it is installed, organized and operated. Studies from both sides of the

Atlantic suggest that VDU operators appear vulnerable to stress-related disorders ranging from insomnia to depression, but this can be blamed more on job dissatisfaction and loss of job security than on such factors as radiation. Monotony and physical isolation seem to make the job less rewarding over time, and a study at Kentucky University found that absenteeism and sickness increased the longer VDU operators were in employment. Fatigue and frustration often result from tasks requiring sustained concentration, and this can only be reduced if operations are carefully planned and appropriate rest pauses introduced. Visual fatigue, and the consequent headaches and sore eyes, seem more likely to result from poor lighting, overcrowding, noise, unsuitable positioning of the terminal, poor supervision, unsuitable work arrangements etc. rather than from the VDU itself. People with sight problems might intensify them by working on VDUs, but this would be true with many other activities. Screen legibility is certainly better on some machines than others, but this is improving all the time and should cease to be a problem. Physical strain (e.g. backache) is similarly more likely to result from a poorly designed work station, with inappropriate furniture etc.

I suspect ergonomics plays a more important part than technology, but to repeat, the evidence to date is inconclusive, and there is no cause for complacency. The conflicting reports perhaps unfortunately allow management often to dismiss symptoms of fatigue and exhaustion as part of the general malaise of clerical workers and representative of their poor work attitude. Women in particular are viewed as 'peripheral workers', exhibiting little company loyalty and high turnover, and scant attention is often paid to health and safety factors in their work. A further problem is that management often expect too much from the technology and are over-demanding on the operators, which intensifies anxiety and depression. The British TUC is concerned over these issues and has demanded 20 minute breaks every 2 hours and regular medical check-ups for VDU operators.

In the United States, there are now over 10 million work stations, and this should grow to 50 million by the end of the 1980s. Unions are demanding legislation to ensure certain standards — good lighting, anti-glare devices, adjustable equipment, regular eye checks and the right of pregnant women to be transferred to alternative work — but so far various business pressure groups have been able to block most proposals, arguing that restrictive laws will stifle technological advancement. In Europe, however, the issue has been less contentious, and many new technology agreements have been introduced.

Job satisfaction

Job satisfaction therefore seems very much the key to health and safety, and it is with this, and the related issue of social relations, that Downing is most concerned. It is often more difficult to obtain firm data, because we are dealing with subjective considerations, and one cannot produce numbers as with labour displacement, or test findings as with health and safety, but it is in these qualitative aspects of work that she believes the effects will most be felt.

Pessimists maintain that when the perpetrators of Taylorism finished changing the factory, they turned their attention to the office and began to significantly divest secretarial workers of control over their work — by mechanizing it, automating it and generally making it more 'efficient'. This involved the introduction of ever more technology and the sub-division of tasks into separate departments — accounts, wages, sales, reprographics etc. Compared to the factory, however, the process remained less advanced. The typewriter, the primary form of office technology, essentially changed little from its invention in 1873, and control of the machine always remained in the hands of the typist. The office remained backward in Taylor's terms because technological application and investment was less, and labour was still largely unregulated, allowing 'costly' periods of 'non-productive' time.

The suggestion is that new information technology will alter this and result in the deskilling of secretarial and other forms of clerical work. In the first place, as we noted in the last chapter, machines like word processors have supervisory and monitoring elements built into them — to check time spent at the machine, work speed, error rates etc. — and transfer control from the typist to the machine itself.

WP operators become wary that comparisons can easily be made between workers which will allow the rates of the faster ones to be imposed on all. In the office, managers have traditionally relied on informal methods of control, and have perhaps even turned a blind eye to workers engaging in non-work activities during working hours. Women workers are usually controlled (by male management) through flattery, praise and encouragement rather than technological surveillance, but this is now destroyed. With the storage of documents in the memory, the secretary no longer has to even move to the filing cabinet, and work can be carried out continuously in front of the machine. All this greatly increases the control management has over the work process and allows for easier checking on quality and output.

Secondly, the word processor can perform all the elementary functions of typing — indenting, centring, tabulating, layout etc. — which can take a person years to perfect. These may seem trivial points, but it has provided the typist with some degree of control, and in a work environment based on flattery and praise, it did provide for some degree of individuality and the recognition of skilled work. (For instance, it has been known for secretaries to develop filing systems which only they can understand so as to create some element of personal indispensability.) Now a less experienced typist — a 'keyboarder' —can produce the same quality of work at much faster speed and considerably less cost. Deskilling is further increased if the printing is done elsewhere and the operator is prevented from seeing her place in the whole work process. Finally, in that the decision over which type of word processing system to install depends on the study of workflow, so office workers become subject to detailed time and motion studies as the office is reorganized and jobs further fragmented.

The introduction of expensive new office technology also means — as in the factory — the likelihood of changed work schedules. Text processors are most cost-effective if used virtually continuously, and this usually means the introduction of shift work and the creation of WP centres akin to the former typing pools. The work may contain less skill and mobility, but still requires high levels of concentration, and as a result operators can feel socially isolated. Studies have found that some workers feel intimidated by the machines; inadequate in understanding what goes on inside them; and perceive such systems as 'unnecessary alien intruders' in the office. Cooper and Cox (1985) found that job satisfaction was significantly higher among traditional secretaries and copy typists than among WP operators. They maintain that this was due to (a) lack of role clarity — over job descriptions, pay scales, job expectations etc. and (b) a feeling of limited career prospects. Other research shows that while secretarial workers may be initially attracted to word processing, especially younger workers who relish the opportunity to operate modern pieces of technology, the 'novelty value' can soon wear off.

Social relations

The office is an area of work where relations between boss and secretary, and between fellow workers, have usually been more personal. It is the destruction of this 'social office' that Downing particularly fears. She maintains that secretarial work, despite the claims of college prospectuses and secretarial manuals, does not have a conventional career structure, and in particular does not facilitate progression from a secretarial position to other branches of management. A secretary's position does not primarily depend on her speeds in shorthand and typing so much as the status of her boss, and becoming secretary to a top director invariably demands other 'feminine' features such as looking the part, smart grooming, refined speech etc. The structure of secretarial work encourages women to be feminine, and consequently for many, especially married women, it is the companionship of other women rather than the content of the job itself that keeps them within the work organization. This reduces alienation and boredom in office work and enables women to develop an informal work culture, which cannot be penetrated by 'masculine' work standards.

Resistance in the form of industrial sabotage, absenteeism, lateness and high labour turnover is often regarded as the preserve of men, but Downing maintains that female office workers also develop their own 'culture of resistance'. Because conventional typewriters rely on the control of the typist, she can adopt any number of strategies to cease working and appear busy when she is not. If work is late, then 'the ribbon got stuck' or she had to call Mr X and couldn't get through. She can leave the typewriter because she has 'run out of paper' or needs something from a file in the other office, where she 'accidentally' meets someone for a chat. She could even perform an act of sabotage by dropping a paper clip into the typewriter and wait for the mechanic to arrive. In short, she has a certain amount of control over her space and movements and, in addition, there are various tasks women are expected to perform simply because they are women, such as making coffee, organizing leaving presents, arranging parties etc. All this enhances her role as 'office wife' but also creates time and space away from the routine of typing.

The pessimists maintain that this will be destroyed by new technology. No longer will the secretary be able to 'create space' and socialize with her fellow female workers, but will be tied for hours on end to her work station. The separation between the conception and execution of work (or the mental/manual division of labour) that Braverman identified is seen as having entered the office as well as the factory and will now intensify due to micro-electronics.

CONCLUSION: OVER-STATING THE EFFECTS

We have here two contrasting views on office work in the future. Guiliano is close to the post-industrial writers in that he adopts a technologically deterministic approach and is optimistic that technology will not only radically, but beneficially, transform the office. He foresees considerable gains in efficiency and cost for employers, and in greater flexibility, variety and job satisfaction for workers. Downing, on the other hand, views these changes within the context of capitalist society and is pessimistic that the office will follow the path of the factory. For her, history shows that tech-nology is not necessarily utilized for the benefit of workers, but only introduced where it costs less than employing human effort and/or enhances managerial control. For the pessimists, the coming of new technology changes little, for the structures of capitalism remain untouched and the deskilling process continues unabated.

My own position is similar to the last chapter. I feel that both sides are over-deterministic and rather underplay the considerable disparities between different installations. Consequently they are each apt to overstate the likely effects of new information technology. Guiliano, for instance, is subject to the criticism that he ignores the political, human context of technological innovation and rather supposes that what could theoretically happen will happen. Admittedly he acknowledges that the information office will not occur overnight, but early signs are that his transitional period might last considerably longer than he seems to think. There are a number of reasons for this which can be summarized under two main headings.

The human factor
The fact that workers can work from home, and hours of work be made more flexible, does not mean it will instantly happen. An experiment by Rank Xerox International, which involved six senior

executives in becoming 'networkers' — working electronically from home — showed that their wives expected them to help more with household chores and that they experienced feelings of low status, especially from neighbours who no longer saw them as doing a 'proper job'. A survey by New York University showed that homeworkers need considerable self-discipline, not just to get their work done, but to combat compulsive eating and smoking. Many suffered considerable stress and needed the gregariousness of the workplace. Teleconferencing systems (which have technically been available for some time through closed-circuit TV) have not sold successfully in the United States because many businessmen apparently prefer to meet face-to-face. Though participation may be wider, the emergence of opinion leaders can be suppressed, thus making the reaching of decisions more difficult. Studies have shown that those who are *not* speaking in a meeting like to be able to pass notes, make faces etc., while those who are prefer to present their arguments in face-to-face situations. In addition, fears have been expressed over confidentiality, and managers appear hesitant to discuss delicate matters over electronic systems.

The management factor

Management, too, may be bothered by the organizational and economic implications of new technology. In the first place, they will not want to bring in flexible work schedules, work from home etc. for employees unless they judge it to be advantageous in terms of control, and economically viable. The cost of much new equipment is still prohibitive, though it is continually falling. Guiliano himself admits that many companies have been slow to embrace the information office and introduce new work patterns, but never questions why this should be. While it is true that word processors are steadily increasing in Britain, the total number is still small, and take-up remains slow overall. This is partly due to the fact that much equipment is still incompatible and, more important, that management is often conservative, unimaginative and non-technological. A survey by BETA Exhibitions Ltd of 500 top UK companies in 1983 found that 50 per cent didn't understand the full potential of office technology, 61 per cent of senior managers still relied on secretaries with shorthand, and 74 per cent admitted they were not effectively using existing office space. Only 57 per cent had one individual charged with purchase responsibility, and in 37 per cent of cases top directors were not involved with purchasing at all. Of those who had introduced new technology, the majority were generally dissatisfied, and more than a quarter of the installations were failing to carry out the function for which they had been purchased. The conclusion was that most companies were not rushing into new technology, and those that were did not seem too sure of what they were doing.

Most managers still prefer existing work arrangements and are anxious to keep their personal secretaries as a status symbol within their work organization. In 1982, only 14 per cent of secretaries were making use of word processors and over 50 per cent of British companies were still making no use of new technology at all. A Manpower Services Commission (MSC) report on central London in 1983 supported an inevitable trend towards word processors, but confirmed that the take-up had been slow and could remain so. For most secretaries, life in 1983 appeared much as it was a decade before, and this was largely due to managers. Clearly, employers' attitudes have to alter, and the technology become more economic, before significant changes can be expected. Due to these various factors, we can expect a considerable 'technological time-lag'. The MSC report found little difference in the nature of work between secretaries who worked with electronic equipment and those who did not, and suggested that technology is less significant than the way secretaries are deployed. The recession has led employers to consider ways of economizing on office staff and one strategy — no doubt adopted reluctantly — has been to organize secretaries so they serve more than one person. In 1970, 70 per cent of secretaries worked for one person only but this had dropped to 50 per cent by 1981. Of course, this move to secretarial 'teams' affects the secretary's status (which is obtained from her boss) and makes the job less 'personal'. Employers now give less emphasis to 'compatibility' in selecting a secretary, while secretaries themselves appear to give less weight to the 'personal relationship'. The declining use of shorthand (51 per cent were using it in 1981 as against 83 per cent in 1970) and its replacement by audio dictation has also reduced personal contact between boss and secretary. Shorthand dictation is inflexible and takes up two people's time while audio dictation and typing is more flexible, if less interesting. WP centres work more effectively with audiotyping, which can mean the operator being plugged in from head to toe.

These developments seem more in line with Downing's predictions, but the point I would stress is that they were already taking place *before* the introduction of word processing (more as a response to economic recession) and not because of it. Leaving aside the fact that new technology may take some time to hit the office, it still seems questionable whether word processing will have as dramatic an effect on secretarial work as pessimists seem to suggest. Mechanization of the office is nothing new and, if not on the same scale as the factory, has steadily increased over the past century. The early mainframe computers encouraged the development of industrial work patterns; clerical tasks have long since been subject to fragmentation and sub-division; and deskilling is already a characteristic feature of much office work. The industrial office is well-established and, in describing the 'social office', Downing seems to rather idealize the secretary's role and under-state the considerable deskilling that has already taken place. Secretarial work has long since been sub-divided, with typists located in their 'pools'. It is *these* employees who are moving to the newly-created WP centres, not the private secretary of the chief executive. Studies have already identified a large degree of dissatisfaction, disappointment and disillusionment with typing roles, and it is questionable to what extent word processing increases this. In short, it seems that the social office was being destroyed well before the advent of microelectronics and that in many instances offices are already a great deal more like factories than the pessimists suggest. In concluding this discussion, we must look at two particularly significant factors: organizational choice and polarization.

Organizational choice
There is no doubt that the effects from office technology can vary according to how firms choose to introduce and organize it, for while some studies show workers disliking word processors, others indicate they prefer the new work situation. The MSC report, for instance, found that word processors were liked by operators and did not have the deskilling effects at first feared. Operators felt the machines freed them from much of the previously repetitive and lengthy typing jobs, allowing more time for other tasks. Some also prefer a work situation where secretaries play a less 'sexist' role and can be judged more by their work output.

Studies suggest that the deskilling effects can be considerably ameliorated by office organization, and this appears to take four main forms:

- The word processing centre — where all correspondence secretaries are located to undertake all typing within the organization.
- Satellite centres — in which both correspondence and administrative secretaries are housed to serve a sub-unit of the organization.
- Back-up centres — providing overload facilities for traditional secretaries.
- A decentralized system — in which word processing facilities are located in normal departments and less division occurs between administrative and correspondence secretaries.

The less centralized the system, it seems, the less the likelihood of deskilling and polarizing secretarial skills. This, of course, is a political decision, not a technical one; a matter for managerial choice. In the Bradford Metropolitan Council installation, the project leader Frank Jones (1981) claimed that he built the system 'from the bottom', meticulously designing it around people and how they preferred to work. The copy typists had no regrets at leaving the typing pool for the WP centre, and over the following two years only three of the twenty-two operators left, compared with an annual turnover rate in the former typing pools of 35 per cent. Jones argues that open-plan industrial offices have long been unpopular with clerical workers and that the pessimists are apt to put a halo round them. He rejects the view that new information technology will depersonalize office relations and believes that 'social space' will be retained as workers invariably 'find a way round' new technology. He believes the major resistance to installations will come from management, who are reluctant to change, invest and innovate, and tend to have a 'top downwards' view of the organization. The fact that other local authorities did not follow Bradford is due, he claims, to the fact that management feel threatened; and, indeed, Jones himself left Bradford because of its 'bureaucratic inertia'. He believes the private sector may prove more responsive, but still expects many managers to be reluctant to dismantle a bureaucracy they've spent twenty years attempting to climb.

WP installations can therefore result in either reskilling or deskilling, and this is largely dependent on organizational choice. Technology itself does not determine a particular job design; managerial values and attitudes still remain the overriding factors.

Polarization

Polarization in terms of skill has occurred in a number of areas and will be discussed more fully in the next chapter, but it is particularly relevant to secretarial work. Many companies have created WP centres, but managers have often by-passed them because they wished to retain their personal secretaries. This has reinforced a growing division between administrative secretaries, who specialize in non-typing secretarial functions, and correspondence secretaries (in the centre), who concentrate solely on typing. This gap could widen further as a result of word processing, and the administrative secretaries — who will still be needed for confidential, non-standard letters, references etc. — come to form an elite. A word processor may be installed in the private secretary's office but, as typing only accounts for around 25 per cent of her duties anyway, she will only resort to it as and when she needs to and, in effect, use it as a typewriter. Standard typing will now go to the word processing operators — the semi-skilled keyboarders — in the WP or satellite centre who will rapidly lose any secretarial skills they once possessed, making the gap between the two groups unbridgeable, and further stunting the growth of any secretarial career ladder. I am suggesting that word processing could further deskill the work of correspondence secretaries (though they have been significantly deskilled already), while the administrative secretaries may not be particularly affected. In other words, the pessimists' scenario could apply to the former group, and the optimists' to the latter. But new information technology may well take a great deal longer to arrive than the optimists imply and, when it does, the deskilling effects may be less dramatic than the pessimists predict. More than anything else, it seems to depend on how the equipment is introduced and organized, and early case studies suggest sweeping generalizations are dangerous.

CHAPTER SIX

The Work Organization

In this chapter we ascend from the workplace level of the factory and office to the corporate level of the work organization as a whole. New information technology is spreading out to affect not just production and 'information' workers, but 'knowledge' workers and all levels of management. In this connection, I shall focus upon different functional areas of management, middle management in general, and computer management in particular, and extend the discussion of polarization introduced at the end of the last chapter.

Since the 1950s, forms of computer technology have altered dramatically, and a major debate has been whether such changes have resulted in greater centralization or decentralization with regard to company structure and management. Again we find that some regard computer technology — and microelectronics in particular — as beneficial to the work organization, not merely administratively and economically, but in human terms. The optimists maintain it will not only remove a great deal of drudgery and repetitiveness from a manager's role, but will encourage greater participation in decision-making at all levels of the organization. New information technology is presented as a democratizing influence in that it decentralizes and spreads power and decision-making. Pessimists, on the other hand, question this and believe it can equally result in more concentrated power at the higher echelons of the organization, the deskilling of middle management, and a greater polarization between high and low management grades. The debate raises many of the issues discussed in previous chapters but particularly highlights the question of 'centralization' and 'decentralization'. To explore this I shall begin with a few words on the development of computer technology and its effect on organizational patterns.

MAINFRAMES AND MINIS

Technologists talk of 'generations' of computers and we are presently in the fourth. The early mainframes of the 1950s were based on valves, which gave way in turn to transistors, integrated circuits and large-scale integrated circuits. The next, fifth generation of computers will be based on very large-scale integration (VLSI) techniques. These dramatic developments have facilitated the manufacture of new forms of computing power, allowed industrial companies to introduce wider applications, and have also resulted in marked changes to the internal structures of large-scale work organizations.

In the 1950s, those companies big enough to be able to justify and afford the early, cumbersome mainframe computers purchased them (as we saw in the last chapter) primarily for data-processing operations. Data would be batched on sheets at various points in the organization and sent to the mainframe to be processed. This created new specialist work tasks, intensified the bureaucratic structure, and undoubtedly had a centralizing effect within companies. As applications needed to be coordinated, the expertise of staff maximized and responsibility for the service located within a particular division, the function had to be centralized. Companies began to create computer services departments — usually consisting of systems analysts, programmers and operators under a computer manager — to take charge of all operations. In larger, multi-site companies, this was usually located at head office so that computer staff developed direct access to senior and top management, and the fact that it was spending considerable sums on the company's behalf also enhanced its prestige and power. Operations also had a centralizing effect, for batch processing did not particularly disrupt the work patterns of lower management and the general clerical staff. In practice, computers were used to solve the problems of the past rather than the future, and little consideration was given to the social and organizational effects that would follow. The computer services department worked in relative isolation at the apex of the organization, providing mainly financial information for senior and top management.

The computer manager was invariably answerable to the financial director. As most of the early applications involved financial procedures — 'event driven' operations such as payroll, purchase and nominal ledger, sales ledger etc. — data processing was usually placed under the accountants. Little thought was given to this choice; it just seemed the natural thing to do. It seemed appropriate, not only that the computer should be initially applied to accounting routines, but that it should be located within the finance department. This was the pattern for the majority of early users and only rarely was the computer attached to other functions such as sales, production or personnel.

This approach, however, had a number of drawbacks. In the first place, the concentration on accounting procedures, which meant the computer was used for *saving* rather than making money, effectively blocked other applications for some time. It also led to computing becoming synonymous with accounting in the eyes of other managers who distanced themselves from applications. Thirdly, it meant that the experience and expertise of computer staff was accumulated from converting well-structured, established procedures, which was to prove unsuitable for later more complex routines requiring a more creative approach. Finally, placing the computer within the accounting function often restricted its political role and meant that the scope of the computer manager to influence senior management remained limited. Many potential users became sceptical of the contribution computers could make to their areas and, overall, the close association between computing and accounting was a barrier to progress. In some instances, the computer manager was promoted to board level, but this was rare.

Early computer services departments were usually sub-divided according to the three main functions — systems analysis, programming and operations — but as this often caused problems in applications development, many companies moved to a project-based structure, with up to half a dozen staff forming a team, which allowed the systems analyst control over all aspects of an installation. Figure 6.1 shows the structure that became the standard form for computer services departments, particularly in medium-size and larger companies.

As computer technology advanced, cheaper minicomputers became available, and batch processing for the mainframe was replaced by on-line terminals. Both developments had a decen-

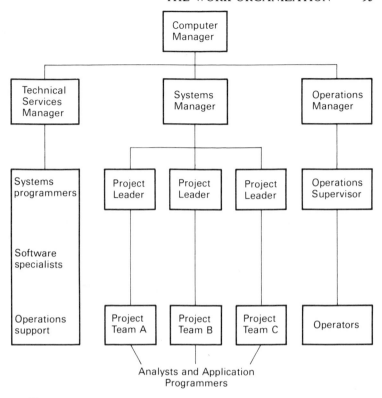

Figure 6.1   Project organization of computer services department
(*Source:* Rowan, 1982)

tralizing effect in that machines could now be purchased at departmental/site level, and general management and staff became directly involved for the first time in the processing of data. No longer was data batched on large sheets and returned to the anonymous central computer department, but was now inputted to terminals at site level. A wider range of staff participated in operations and a greater volume of data generated within the organization. This increase in installations made the structure over-complex in some instances — as a greater divide occurred between production activities and specialist support services — and some companies created separate administration sections or moved towards more elaborate management services departments. These incorporated organization and method, operations research etc., as well as the computer which now became seen as one of several tools available to management.

THE MICROCOMPUTER

The coming of the microcomputer has had a further — and far more significant — decentralizing effect on the work organization, for it has placed the equivalent power of an early mainframe (at a modest price) on the desk of every manager. It can be used, not only for accounting applications, but for stock control, sales orders, production planning etc., and thereby reduces management's dependency on a centrally-based computer services department. Such changes have made the department, in its conventional form, obsolete. In 1982, over a dozen of the largest UK companies broke up their central divisions and established the trend towards 'distributive processing' whereby computer specialists are dispersed to various points of the organization. Here they are (significantly) re-titled business analysts rather than systems analysts and perform an advisory role, assisting managerial colleagues with small-scale installations.

The site manager is now demanding five main things. First, he is increasingly wanting information available at site level; he is less willing to wait for the next run of his work or on distant programmers for special reports. Secondly, he requires selectivity; a database which will arrange his information requests and retrieve and arrange answers. Thirdly, he needs swift responses, for the commercial world is increasingly competitive. Fourthly, he wants control over his system, partly because of his difficulties with computer staff in the past. Finally, he requires advice and guidance as the computer world is changing so quickly. Many companies now feel these needs can be more easily met through a decentralized structure.

This is not to suggest that the central computer department will totally disappear, for it can still perform certain functions more effectively; namely, project management skills, equipment and software selection, central quality control, skills in 'frontier areas' (e.g. telecommunications, databases etc.) and identifying needs within the organization. But it will exist in a modified and narrower

Table 6.1   Generations of computer development

Changes in computer technology	Changes in computer applications	Changes in computer organization
1. Valves 1945–54	Batch processing on mainframe	Finance department
2. Transistors 1954–65	On-line processing to mainframe	Computer services — function based
3. Integrated circuits 1965–	Minicomputer with terminals	Computer services — project based
4. Large-scale integrated circuits 1972–	Microcomputer	Distributive processing
5. Very large-scale integration	Microcomputers in integrated information network	

form. Similarly, the company mainframe will not suddenly vanish (for it is still more efficient for operations like payroll), but will be supplemented by a growing arsenal of other machines. The various changes we have considered in this section — in computer technology, applications and organization — can be summarized as in Table 6.1.

It is not suggested that these 'generational stages' are distinct and precise, with clear-cut lines of demarcation between them: I am painting with a 'broad brush' and the stages should rather be seen as approximate and overlapping. In the United States, for instance, the time-scale would be some way in advance of Britain, while the length of the developmental time-span will vary between companies. In general, the widespread purchase of microcomputers by management seems more likely in large companies manufacturing a wide range of products on multiple sites, who invested in computing facilities at an early stage for a wide range of applications, and established a central computer services department. Because of their size, and the need to delegate financial accountability, these companies also invariably operate a decentralized policy for purchasing, which encourages managers to invest in their own machines.

THE DECENTRALIZING ARGUMENT

The optimists welcome the arrival of the microcomputer and the accompanying decentralizing move to distributive processing on a number of counts. They see the micro as a tool for *all* managers, and feel that computer specialists are more effectively employed if assisting colleagues with small-scale installations. There are many advantages in developing such systems. Operation and processing at the point of activity can assist system maintenance, and files can be updated as new products and other developments arise. There is a considerable cost saving, and greater interest and support should be generated among management and operators (who see it more as *their* system). The picture is one of computer technology operating at all points of the organizational pyramid, allowing every manager to make far quicker and more effective decisions in an increasingly complex and competitive industrial situation.

The technology is therefore viewed as a democratizing force within companies, for more information is available throughout the organization; more managers participate in decision-making; and overall organizational effectiveness is enhanced. Individual managers can, with the assistance of computer staff, build up small-scale installations which, if they prove successful, can be linked to form a chain, and the company moves towards an integrated information circuit. All this provides a totally new climate within work organizations. Whereas the mainframe approach required one to think in *vertical* (and hierarchical) terms — from head office machine down to on-line terminals — with the microcomputer one has to think horizontally, in terms of a series of small-scale micro systems developed across a company. All this makes organizational operations more open, fluid and flexible, and allows skilled managers — Bell's 'technocrats' — to operate with greater effectiveness in a more egalitarian atmosphere.

This move from vertical to horizontal operations is described in the work of Alvin Toffler. He argues that because of new information technology, conventional organizational hierarchies are collapsing. Bureaucracies — which rank people hierarchically and separate decision-makers from others — are being altered, side-stepped and broken down; organizations are forced to change their internal structures to accommodate temporary units as 'sideways' becomes as important as 'up and down'.

Bureaucratic decision-making, says Toffler, invariably goes through a series of vertical stages, which accounts for why it is so notoriously slow, rigid and inefficient. It may well be suitable for solving routine problems at a moderate pace, but it becomes manifestly inappropriate when things are speeded up and less routine. The pace of technological change is now so fast that every minute of 'down time' costs more in lost output than ever before; information must flow through the organization swiftly to meet increasing competition; more information is needed to deal with non-routine problems; those lower in the hierarchy must take more decisions to avoid the delays of 'red tape'; and horizontal communication increases as workers make greater use of specialists (e.g. computer experts) and immediate colleagues.

Toffler maintains that it will be some time before bureaucracy is obliterated because it is well suited to routine tasks, and plenty of these still remain. However, it is precisely these tasks that computers can increasingly do better. Automation therefore ultimately leads to the overthrow of bureaucracy. Bureaucracies also stifle the imaginative and creative qualities managers now need in solving non-routine problems. He points out that wherever organizations are concerned with technological change, where research and development is prominent, and where problems are non-routine, the decline of bureaucracy is most pronounced.

For such optimists, bureaucracy is the form of organization for an industrial age: it was not needed in pre-industrial times and is inappropriate for post-industrial society. In future, problems will be solved by task forces composed of 'relative strangers who represent a set of diverse professional skills'. Executives and senior managers will function as coordinators for these various teams, and people will be differentiated, not vertically according to rank and role, but horizontally, according to skill and professional training. There will be greater mobility between teams and less group cohesiveness, as managers take their expertise where needed and obtain greater job satisfaction from applying their particular skills to specific problems.

This leads Toffler to conclude that bureaucracy is being replaced by 'ad-hocracy' and 'organization man' by 'associate man'. He identifies three key features of bureaucracy:

● permanence (in which the organization endures through time)

- hierarchy (in which the individual knows his ranking)
- division of labour (in which the individual occupies a well-defined niche)

and argues that these are now being replaced by transience, mobility and flexibility, respectively. The bureaucratic manager, faced with routine problems, was encouraged to provide routine answers, and unorthodoxy, creativity and imagination were discouraged. In the ad-hocracy, people operate in a constant state of flux, moving round within organizations and even between them. In this meritocratic society, people become more loyal to their specialism than an organization — cosmopolitans rather than locals, and task-orientated rather than job-orientated.

Toffler also perceives a rise in entrepreneurship, albeit in a new form. Because of the increasing affluence made available by new information technology and the security provided by the welfare state, managers become more prepared to experiment and apply their skills and imagination. 'Associate man' represents a new kind of entrepreneur for the post-industrial age (Table 6.2).

In taking Toffler as representative of the optimistic, decentralizing view, it is interesting to note how similar his discussion is to that of Bell. While Bell focuses on society rather than the work organization, they both talk in similar terms of post-industrial change, and stress the role of technology in this development. They emphasize the growing importance of knowledge, the rise of technocrats and the greater use of computers in decision-making. Most important, they see this leading to a more open, fluid, meritocratic and democratic society — both within the organization and without — in which old-style class divisions dissolve and people are allocated tasks according to their expertise. In such an atmosphere, exploitation and conflict give way to teamwork and harmony.

In a sense, any form of computerized system has an 'unveiling' and thereby democratizing effect, for the logic of computer-based systems is to encourage open and equal access to information, as managers are forced to express decision processes explicitly so that they can be handled by software programs. But as Crozier (1983) points out, this may not result in practice, for new technology has to be introduced into *existing* organizations. Managers have power bases they wish to protect, and technological change cuts right

Table 6.2

Organization man	Associate man
Subservient to the organization	Owes only temporary loyalty to the organization
Immobile — fears for security	Mobile — takes economic security for granted
Fearful of risk	Welcomes risk
Seeks prestige within the organization; conscious of hierarchy	Seeks prestige without the organization
Fills predetermined slot	Moves from slot to slot in a pattern that is largely self-motivated
Solves routine problems according to well-defined rules	Solves novel problems with ill-defined rules
Orthodox and conventional	Creative and innovative
Subordinates individuality	Only temporarily subordinates individuality to a particular team
Seeks permanent relations	Accepts temporary relations

across the established hierarchical, bureaucratic structure of which they are a part. In short, computers come to disturb the very decision-making procedures they are supposed to assist. Again we need to consider the political and human context, for if managers feel they are being forced to change (and feel their power base threatened) they will cling to established procedures. This may include top management who become reluctant to release information that has traditionally been their prerogative. In this scenario, the computer becomes superimposed on an existing framework which reinforces the *status quo* and ossifies conservative forms of decision-making. While managers might expect computers to 'magically' deal with complexity, in practice they add to it, and can act as an agent for consolidation rather than change. It is for these reasons that some commentators see new technology as a force for greater centralization.

THE CENTRALIZING ARGUMENT

Pessimists would maintain that while there has clearly been a growth in horizontal communication, this has not been at the *expense* of vertical communication: there has simply been growth in all forms of inter-organizational activity as work operations have become increasingly complex. It is not a zero-sum situation in which the former replaces the latter, and as Blau and Schoenherr (1973) point out, paradoxically we are freer today from coercion through the power of superiors, yet at the same time people in positions of power probably exercise greater power than any tyrant ever has.

This point should be kept in mind during the following discussion. But first, a few words on 'centralization' and 'decentralization'. The difference between the two involves a tension between efficiency and flexibility. All organizations want to prove efficient while still remaining flexible, but these two concerns often stand opposed to each other. Efficiency can be greatly enhanced by centralization, for concentrating decision-making in the hands of top executives improves coordination, maximizes expertise, economizes on managerial overheads, locates responsibility and involves fewer people. Its weakness, however, is that as a strategy of control it can easily appear authoritarian and inflexible, may not always be available or appropriate, and can easily prove counterproductive. Consequently, many companies have been attracted to the decentralized approach for this enhances flexibility; allows swifter decisions from those closer to the action; brings the profit motive to bear on a wider group; and (supposedly) provides greater motivation, wider democracy and more effective use of expertise.

An important point must be made. It should not be thought that a decentralized structure implies a weak centre; it is simply an *alternative* mechanism for maintaining control, only operates on terms laid down by the centre, and is still control. It is maintained, not by centralizing decisions towards the top, but by setting clearly prescribed tasks, rules and procedures within which people can operate. This less visible form of power sets limits on what subordinates might do, and provides a kind of freedom of manoeuvre within bounds; but it is still bureaucratic control.

It may therefore be misleading to suggest that with decentralization we necessarily witness some kind of movement in power terms from the centre to the periphery, or from the top to the bottom. Certainly with microcomputers more processing can be done at all points of the organization, and this may well involve increasing use of horizontal communication, but none of this need mean that centralized, bureaucratic control is reduced, let alone removed. On the contrary, far from new information technology passing greater decision-making powers to lower levels, it can as easily be used to provide greater central control throughout the organization.

It is therefore dangerous to suggest that microcomputers must enhance organizational democracy. Technological change clearly has implications for organizational structure, but while microcomputers may allow — or even encourage — more participative procedures, there is no certainty they will ensure it. In the first place, there will always be some centralizing tendencies. For instance, in large companies it is doubtful whether a totally decentralized computing operation — in which managers indiscriminately purchase whatever equipment they wish — could ever be justified long-term by top management. There are indications that many companies allow individual purchases for some time — to encourage familiarity with new technology — but then impose purchasing restrictions to ensure a coherent strategy in terms of compatibility and costs.

But, more important, top management may prefer to use new information technology to enhance their own position rather than disperse organizational decision-making. In this connection, we should not think of microcomputers as operating in isolation, for they can be linked with each other and to a centralized mainframe to provide instant information from all parts of the company. Any 'time-lag' problems are overcome, and centralization enhanced, in that those at the organizational summit can now more tightly observe every aspect of the company's operations. A chief executive can sit in his exclusive penthouse office and electronically check, not only on whether a particular worker has spent too long on a coffee break or a typist is working up to speed, but whether a middle manager is performing as he should be. In short, the flexibility offered by decentralization is also available to top executives and allows re-centralization to occur: central control and freedom of action for decentralized units can co-exist. What pessimists suggest is that if the microcomputer encourages any form of decentralization, it is only in a restricted, *technological* sense. Computer applications become increasingly feasible at ever lower levels of the organization, but this need not mean all control and decision-making pass to these levels. We need to distinguish the quantity of decisions from the quality: the fact that people are using new technology to make *more* decisions does not mean they are decisions of greater importance. While technology may move down in organizational terms, control can move up (Fig. 6.2).

In terms of management control, new technology can thus increase central control within a decentralized structure. But we return to our central theme. There is no technical reason why this *has* to happen; microcomputers do not *necessarily* result in either greater centralization or decentralization. Computer technology does not determine the shape and nature of work organizations: it may suggest certain forms of structure, but it cannot impose. The outcome depends on the particular company and is a matter for managerial choice.

New information technology could certainly be used to facilitate more effective delegation and greater participation from both staff and management: this could be done by plugging each local unit into a common file system so that they have access to all company information. Increased centralization also runs contrary to much research on motivation, participation, industrial democracy etc., but studies suggest most companies are unlikely to follow the decentralization path. Child refers to research into electronic-point-

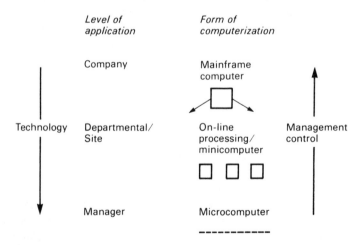

Figure 6.2   Computer technology and centralization/decentralization

of-scale (EPOS) systems in retailing where the more precise information has been used, not to provide wider information access for all staff, but to extend centralized control over ordering decisions, stock levels, size of labour establishment, in-store performance etc. My own work at a biscuit factory, where large numbers of terminals were available to all ranks of personnel, revealed that hardware was 'doctored' so that only certain data was retrievable at each level. The VDU operators were granted minimal discretion and felt less control over data than in their previous work situations. Staff found themselves working long hours at terminals; offices were re-arranged, making communication with colleagues difficult; and working to a distant mainframe intensified feelings of isolation and detachment. In general, they preferred their previous work which they felt provided greater responsibility, variety, interest and satisfaction. My experience is that it is difficult to view computer technology as some kind of 'emancipator' at the base of most work organizations.

The pessimists conclude that decentralization should not be viewed as in some way synonymous with democracy, though many top managers are apt to make this connection. To bring the profit motive and other responsibilities to bear on lower levels, and to provide them with new technology, may prove stimulating and motivating, but does not make fully participative management automatic. A particular form of computer technology is not more or less likely to result in decentralized management, nor is a decentralized structure necessarily conducive to wider democratic participation. Such factors depend on the strategy of management, for a decentralized structure can equally be used to maintain strong central control. Decentralization may *disperse* control, but it need not *dilute* it: and computer technology can prove a powerful tool in this process.

POLARIZATION

The conclusion we reach is similar to that of the previous two chapters. While the optimists suggest new technology will rejuvenate the work situation, re-skill tasks, upgrade work and provide greater participation, the pessimists fear further deskilling through automation and an increasing polarization between those with high-grade technological skills and those with no real skills at all.

Given that this process can be identified in certain instances in the factory and office, is it also applicable to management? Can the very people responsible for introducing and administering new information technology themselves become subject to its deskilling effects? In this final section, I wish to return and look more closely at the question of job polarization. A number of writers have, in their different ways, proposed a dual model of the work enterprise which suggests that the top part of the organizational pyramid is structurally different from the bottom part (Fig. 6.3). While the top sector corresponds to Weber's bureaucratic model, in which employees are provided with a vertical career structure through hierarchical grades, the bottom part is increasingly constructed according to Taylor's principles of scientific management whereby people are arranged horizontally into simple, manual, specialized, repetitive jobs. The separation between the conception and execution of work is intensified as control of the work situation passes from the worker to those higher in the organization, and work in factory and office is increasingly deskilled.

Those above the organizational divide tend to have a more 'diffuse implicit contract' in which they are required to use discretion in their work, maintain high trust relations with their superiors, and think in terms of careers. Those below the divide — in manual and, increasingly, routine clerical and service work — are characterized by a 'restricted implicit contract'. Here, work tasks are more closely prescribed and executed on the basis of a contractual commitment which is specific rather than diffuse; relationships with superiors are low trust; there is little potential career promotion; and workers are paid wages rather than salaries.

This model can also be applied to the changing position of management, and helps synthesize the debate as to whether professional managers are becoming more important with the growth of the 'knowledge society' or are 'proletarianized' as their work becomes increasingly deskilled within work organizations. The model suggests both processes can occur simultaneously depending on whether particular skills can be routinized, sub-divided or taken over by a machine. This can be seen in the case of personnel, where a separation has occurred between the position of foreman and personnel manager, or accountancy, where book-keeping has been relegated in status while others exercise discretion and judgement as finance executives. This polarization is not dissimilar to the one

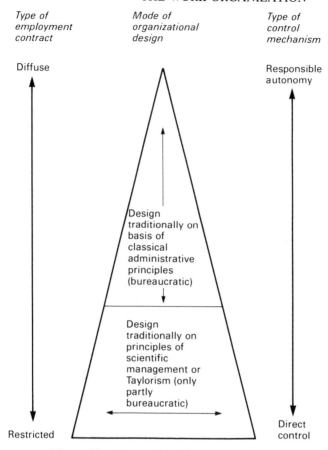

Figure 6.3   *Two modes of organizational design*
(*Source:* Watson, 1980)

we discussed in the previous chapter between administrative and correspondence secretaries.

Are other areas of management now likely to experience this process, especially as a result of new information technology? Pessimists would claim that the model usefully shows how all branches of middle management could be affected.

● It will move the boundary line between the two sectors of the organization — between planning and performance — upwards. Just as planning was taken from the skilled worker, so it will now be taken from middle managers. Technology will take over supervision, record and process information and, finally, transmit that information. Their numbers could contract (as Jenkins and Sherman predict) while those who remain find themselves relegated to the lower parts of the organization.

● Large organizations will recentralize as top managers take on a greater planning role. The former planning tasks of middle managers are now transferred to the higher echelons of the company.

● The line separating the two parts of the organization will be drawn more clearly. Fewer people will be needed, and managers will find it difficult to retrain and readjust.

● All managers will make greater use of computer technology but for many this will result in repetitive, mundane tasks, and a fall in terms of skill, status and pay.

Some optimists would oppose this on the grounds that it underestimates the full role of management, which is still to negotiate, conciliate, inspire and lead. Managers often have to base decisions on information that is unsystematic, diverse and fragmented, and within increasingly complex modern work organizations, management — at all levels — remains an art that is not easily superseded by technology.

Pessimists, however, insist that a major part of middle management's role is the collection, interpretation and distribution of information, and because this can now be done so swiftly and efficiently by new technology, their position could become largely redundant. This will mean a reduction in the ranks of middle management, a contraction of hierarchical grades, and a slimming of staff and support roles below the strategic level.

We have not quite finished, for the pessimists would also claim that this process has, with the break-up of computer services departments, even hit the computer specialists themselves — the very people who brought in the technology that deskilled others. Ironically, they fall victim to their own devices. Braverman argues that computer work, which for a short period up to 1960 displayed the characteristics of a craft with workers performing a number of different functions, has been sub-divided into a hierarchy of separate tasks. The increasing availability of packaged software and high-level languages has allowed the status of programmers to be lowered and this is now extending to systems analysts and computer managers as hardware developments permit each manager a personal computer. Skills can be routinized, sub-divided or taken over by the machine itself, which means computer staff are relegated within the organization.

Without doubt, recent developments have adversely affected career patterns for many computer specialists. From a period of sustained growth over two decades — during which time they had the protection of head office and a strong central department around them — they have moved into an uncertain climate in which they are dispersed as 'consultants' to advise other managerial colleagues on individual applications. Consequently, computer managers have not generally joined top management but have in most cases remained answerable to the financial director. Not that other managers have shown much distress at these happenings. Computer staff have generally been distrusted by their colleagues because they acquired (in a remarkably short space of time) a central position in the political framework of the organization and exercised considerable power over all aspects of operations. The computer department retained a monopolistic hold over its function (through the mainframe) and was not dependent on other departments or substitutable by them. While other branches of management (e.g. accountants, personnel etc.) emerged to occupy central positions within organizations, they rarely created such levels of antagonism because they provided a service *to the organization* but did not require other managers to adjust. Computer services provided a service *to other managers* which demanded adjustments on their part, and it was this — especially when the service was thought to be of poor quality — that caused resentment.

The re-emergence of powerful computer services departments seems unlikely, for they would be politically resisted by other sections of management. Accountants, production managers, general managers, and even top managers, have clawed back ground lost to computer specialists and will not easily relinquish it. The power of the specialist department has been diluted in two main ways: first by deskilling the lower levels of computer work (e.g. programming) and, secondly, by incorporating the upper echelons (e.g. the systems analysts) into general management. The computer services department should remain, but its role and powers will be significantly altered.

CHAPTER SEVEN

Citizenship

If the optimists and pessimists, in their different ways, both predict such dramatic changes in the work situation as a result of new information technology, then it is hardly surprising that they expect the effects to spill over into the non-work situation. In this and the following chapter, I shall therefore broaden the debate, and for that matter the technology, to embrace the issue of citizenship and life in the home. How will our lives be affected by the fact that more information is available, not only to our employers, but to politicians, the police, the medical profession — even ourselves?

New information technology makes vast amounts of information available, at staggering speed, to all sorts of people. Much of this will be straightforward factual material, such as information on theatre tickets or train times, but it will also include more personal information such as medical or work records. A hundred years ago, few records were kept — apart from births, marriages and deaths — but now data is held on social security, taxation, education, employment and a host of other subjects. Clearly such a transformation has enormous implications for life in democratic society, and for individual citizenship.

The key question is: do such changes enhance the liberties of the individual, or are they more appropriately seen as mechanisms restricting personal freedom? We can again divide between optimists and pessimists; between those who welcome the *expansion* of new technology and information for the administrative benefits it provides, and those anxious to *protect* the democratic rights, liberties and privacy of individuals. I shall at times label these two groups the 'expansionists' and 'protectionists', and consider their contrasting viewpoints on citizenship with reference to the central issues of representative democracy and personal privacy. The first addresses the wider concerns of the political system as a whole, while the second focuses down to the rights of the individual citizen.

REPRESENTATIVE DEMOCRACY

In Western industrialized society, we hold great store by 'democratic values' and to the view that democracy is a 'good thing'. It is the fact that our political system is 'democratic' that distinguishes it from the military dictatorships of South America or the communist regimes of Eastern Europe, and this ideal is shared by most political figures in Britain, whatever their particular shade. The right-wing conservative will voice the 'democratic virtues' of individual freedom just as the left-wing socialist will call for the 'democratic rights' of equality, opportunity and justice. But what does 'democracy' mean? It could be argued that the system with which we are familiar in fact takes a very imperfect form and that, despite the extension of 'one man, one vote', we have in many respects moved further away from true democracy. The notion of a 'city state', in which all citizens join together in true democratic fashion to pursue their political deliberations, becomes quite impossible in an industrialized society of some 57 million. Consequently we have adopted a 'representative', or 'parliamentary', form of democracy whereby citizens form into constituencies; elect individuals to represent them in various assemblies; and only indirectly influence political decision-making.

This ceases to be true democracy in a number of respects. In the first place, the member once elected is more a representative than a delegate, bound by the views of his party rather than his constituents. There are also many instances where members, even governments, do not pursue the policies and views they advocated at the time of election. Thirdly, and this particularly applies to Britain, there is often little relationship between the allocation of parliamentary seats to particular political parties and the total votes cast. In the 1983 election, although the SDP/Liberal Alliance received 26 per cent of the vote to Labour's 28 per cent, they secured 186 fewer seats and, more important, the victorious Conservative Party received the support of less than half those who voted, and less than a third of the total electorate, but was returned with an overall majority of 144. The alternative of proportional representation (PR) could create equivalent problems, for it is mathematically more complex; may well involve a series of elections; is slow producing a result; removes the single-member constituency; and invariably results in coalition governments being secretly formed in smoke-filled rooms. Does the coming of new information technology therefore have any implications for representative democracy?

Cable systems
Post-war politics has already been dramatically affected by a new technology — television. Television has made politics more immediate, more visual and more personal; it has changed the kinds of faces, voices and personalities that win elections. This could once more be re-shaped by the coming of cable systems and the provision of over thirty channels to people's homes. The effect of this would be for broadcasting to be largely replaced by 'narrowcasting', which has considerable implications for the presentation of politics. Up to now, politicians have used television to send short, general messages to large audiences, but this would now be replaced by longer messages to smaller audiences. Many countries already provide live coverage of national parliaments, and in the United States various cable systems show city council meetings. Longer, more detailed presentations could now be broadcast for minority groups such as Roman Catholics, Devonians, the unemployed, or whoever. As technology becomes cheaper yet more widespread, so it would have a special impact upon local elections, and viewers could become as familiar with their councillor or member of parliament as they are with national political figures. In addition, local interest groups would be able to broadcast in the free time usually available on cable systems.

Optimists argue that this is encouraging. New technology should provide greater access to the electorate, particularly for poorer candidates and minority groups; live television coverage should make politicians more responsive to the electorate than to powerful lobbies; and it should generally increase public participation in politics.

There is, however, another side. While such developments may appear as a stimulant to democracy, it must be remembered that the potential television audience is now dissected across thirty separate channels, and pessimists fear we may end up with smaller and smaller groups knowing more and more about less and less. There is also the fear that those interest groups with largest resources will be able to buy greater influence through the cable networks, certainly for the foreseeable future. Moreover, as politics becomes more interwoven with entertainment and commercialism, the worry is that it will become increasingly trivialized and polluted. Narrowcasting may fragment our perception of events, encouraging us to pursue news items that interest us in detail to the neglect of others. But this would be no different from the situation that appertains to newspapers, where we already choose to read those stories that interest us (or those newspapers that interest us), and the small number of cable viewers watching a city council meeting would almost certainly be in excess of those attending in person.

Electronic polling

An even more dramatic change could occur with regard to polling. A hint of what to expect comes from the experiments in local democracy that have operated through the QUBE system in such 'wired' cities as Columbus, Ohio. The system has now been extended to Cincinnati, Pittsburgh, Houston, Dallas and Omaha, and offers thirty channels of cable television and various two-way communication services such as electronic shopping, information services, home security services and voter participation (*see* Chapter 8). The latter operates by subscribers attaching a small black box containing several buttons to their television set, and tapping in their particular preferences.

The television announcer poses the question, the viewer selects from four choices, and the result appears on the screen within seconds. Initially this was largely restricted to fairly flippant decisions over quiz shows and soap opera endings (in which viewers could vote for a sad, happy or 'come back next week' ending) but it is also used for local political issues. The city's mayor, a local school board chairman, or whoever, can present a case for a particular policy and a referendum of the whole electorate be instantly taken.

In the United States, it is calculated that by 1990 up to a quarter of the population could have such facilities, and this clearly removes many of the shortcomings to representative democracy that we mentioned earlier. The case against PR, for instance, is significantly weakened because mathematical complexity is now no obstacle (second preferences etc. can be handled instantaneously) and the time-consuming element of conventional vote counting is removed. But the technology does more than this for it raises a question mark over the whole system of representative democracy — in whatever form — as we know it. Optimists welcome the new technology as a truly democratizing force which allows the city state (or even nation state) to re-appear. Masuda terms this 'participatory democracy' and believes people will demand more involvement as political decisions have an increasing influence on their lives. He envisages a society in which all citizens are equipped with home terminals (which have become increasingly cheap) and are given the opportunity to vote on particular issues. For instance, it might be decided that at seven o'clock on a Friday evening, the entire nation could vote as to whether or not it wished to restore capital punishment. The vote could be preceded by a full-scale debate and the result known in seconds. Such a system would dramatically affect the role of elected representatives as we know them and logically encourage wider electoral participation.

The pessimists, however, are less enthusiastic. The returns in Columbus are certainly biased in that poorer people are less likely to be subscribers and are therefore deprived of a vote. In addition, one cannot be exactly sure who has voted: do we want a four-year-old or a dog deciding over comprehensive education? It could further be argued that such systems tend to measure people's immediate response to a problem and do not encourage deliberation and analysis. Swift decisions on the Irish question, for instance, would almost certainly prove non-beneficial. It might also be asked why voters are offered four, and only four, choices when there may be various other alternatives. Four options may be convenient for the technology, but it could well result in political over-simplification. Even with four alternatives, the way the question is posed may also determine the outcome (as many say happened with the only referendum Britain has ever undertaken, on whether to leave the Common Market). Most important of all, who decides on the four alternatives and how they are worded? Active political participation in instant referenda could well benefit existing power structures more than citizens.

While electronic polling may strengthen the *vertical* links —

between citizen and decision-maker — it could simultaneously weaken *horizontal* links between sub-groups — local parties, pressure groups, work groups, families etc. — which, it might be argued, represent the true heart of democracy. The picture becomes one of individuals confronting and deciding issues in isolation, and as they become *less* organized, so power increasingly passes to existing bureaucratic hierarchies. The information is now used by power holders to *predict* public reaction — which enables them to circumvent it more easily — and if citizens fear their opinions are not just being listened to, but also recorded and analysed electronically, this could lead to higher rather than lower levels of political apathy. With conventional elections, although voting is secret, it is done *in public* and it is this that enables us to ensure secrecy. We might replace free voting in public with coerced voting in private (e.g. with key family members imposing their views on others). And finally, some see dangers for a society over-dependent on computerized systems: a breakdown of such systems (or their sabotage by powerful groups) makes a democratic society highly vulnerable.

Once more it is argued that technology can be both beneficial and harmful. The gains of access, immediacy, participation and visibility — so welcomed by the optimists — are counter-balanced by the pessimists' fear of superficiality, simplification, indoctrination and triviality. While new information technology may expand opportunities for political participation, it could equally threaten democratic rights that need to be protected.

PRIVACY

Of equal concern is the delicate issue of privacy. As the power of computers has increased, so the electromagnetic storing of data has gained in popularity. With cheap microcomputers and improvements in telecommunications, systems can now hold and process vast amounts of data and make it available on VDUs based many miles away. The optimists would stress that this offers many advantages in our daily lives. They value the new technology for the administrative benefits it provides and believe that the gains will far outweigh any drawbacks. The claim is that the expansion of new technology and information will generally inform, improve and invigorate our democratic society.

Large data-processing computers are already integrated into national and international networks, and central government departments, local authorities, the police, social services, financial institutions and employers all make use of computerized systems for holding data on individuals. It is not always realized just how extensive these now are. In Britain today, two government departments alone — the Home Office and the Department of Health and Social Security (DHSS) — hold no less than 113 million personal records stored in thirty-two separate computer systems, covering vehicle owners, TV licences, blood groups, prison records, employment benefit etc.

Most data held is in no way sinister, and helps meet the needs of both data user and data subject. For instance, data held on my bank account is of use both to me and my bank manager, and it is in both our interests that it is accurate, accessible and not obtainable by others. Indeed, in the field of banking it is questionable whether modern financial institutions could now cope without computers, for they have greatly eased the arranging of credit and processing of cheques as financial transactions have increased in complexity.

Similarly, the better the records of the DHSS or the vehicle registration centre, the more this benefits both these departments and the individual citizen. Welfare benefits can be distributed more equitably and efficiently as computers take over clerical chores and allow officials more time to examine individuals' claims and problems. Systems can provide the public with a much improved service as the important (but often repetitive) demands of the unemployed, sick and elderly are handled by technology. In Cardiff and Brighton, for instance, experiments have already been tried in which computers 'enquire' about claimants' circumstances and suggest benefits to which they are entitled. Optimists claim that the gains from such developments are considerable.

Pessimists, however, take a contrasting view and maintain that, far from enhancing democracy, new technology poses a direct challenge to it. They insist that the overriding importance is to *protect* the privacy and personal liberties of the individual citizen. This addresses two main issues. In the first place, they are concerned over the ability of the state (and others) to 'spy' on an individual through new technological devices. British Telecom's System X telephone exchange system, for instance, is designed to allow 'official' telephone tapping, and specific calls can be routed to special centres run by the Home Office or British Telecom. Similarly, the interactive cable system discussed earlier would not only allow citizens to voice their various preferences, but could equally serve governmental and private agencies with data on people's political opinions, buying habits, financial status, leisure activities, and family and friends. Other data banks could supply sensitive information on religious beliefs, medical records, employment history or criminal activity. This view approximates to George Orwell's vision of 1984 in which, it will be recalled, Big Brother and the party were able through two-way telescreens to 'switch in' and invade all aspects of Winston Smith's personal life. Such a situation is not unrealistic, for laser systems can now pick up conversations over half a mile away through processing the vibrations of a window pane, and electronic bugging devices have become increasingly sophisticated.

The second concern relates to the accessibility that individuals have to data held on them. Protectionists would argue that access to such data is a fundamental right in a democratic society. Data kept on individuals may be purely factual; may seem fairly innocuous; may lie dormant for years; and may offer no particular threat to the individual's liberty, but this does not answer the point that the individual has the right to know of such data. The main danger, of course, is that data users may prove incompetent, may misconstrue their own interests, or may simply be devious and criminal. In such circumstances, computerized systems do not work for but rather against the interests of the private citizen. Data held may be inaccurate, available to unauthorized persons or used for improper purposes, such fears being particularly prevalent in the case of police and medical records. The fear is that those in power, far from becoming more answerable to the general populace, may use technology to maintain and enhance their control. The machine takes on an 'objectivity' which never existed in the case of the official, and the citizen feels he has little recourse against decisions it imposes. Rather like the lie-detector, the computer acquires a mantle of scientific infallibility that is by no means always justified.

It is this scenario with its accompanying violation of civil liberties that causes concern, especially as more information of an increasingly delicate and personal nature becomes available. This view is therefore more concerned with privacy than efficiency, to protect individual liberties rather than boost the effectiveness of state administration.

Cross-referencing

Expansionists are more optimistic and question why there is so much concern about computerized data. After all, the retention of personal records is nothing new: the sheer complexity of modern industrialized society has meant that for years governmental and other institutions have collected information on members of the public, and this has been generally accepted. Record systems have long existed in manual form and, in principle, computerized systems are no different. There is simply *more* data on *more* people and this added complexity, it is argued, if anything assists anonymity and privacy.

Tapper (1983) optimistically maintains that the dangers from computerized systems are no greater than those that exist already, and that computers get a 'bad press' simply because any shortcomings are far more visible. It is in fact easier, he argues, to ensure that data in computer systems is complete and accurate as automatic checks and warnings can be incorporated. He rejects the notion that the computer has somehow converted good uses of personal information into evil uses; if this is so, the fault lies with the operators, not the machine.

But why have the protectionists expressed such fear and suspicion? The central concern is that with computers, data can be processed at virtually any distance, vast amounts can be stored and (most important) different indexes can be cross-referenced. This last point allows separate sets of data, probably collected for totally different purposes, to be correlated and, in effect, allows data to be turned into new information. With a computer, the data previously held on various sheets of paper in different filing cabinets throughout a range of different departments can be correlated into a comprehensive dossier in a matter of seconds. It was the natural constraints of the manual system that provided the protection for our privacy: manual systems can only take so much data before they become unworkable and, consequently, only the most important data is selected for storage. With a computer, the amount of data that can be stored is virtually unlimited and the tendency is to retain information that is irrelevant, outdated or even inaccurate. The concern is a simple one: it is perfectly acceptable that our doctor should have access to our medical records, but not necessarily an employer or the tax man. Similarly, while the tax man may know of our financial circumstances, we may not wish these to be available to family and friends. So long as information is dispersed between different agencies, our privacy is preserved: cross-referencing on a computer can destroy this.

The situation becomes particularly worrying if citizens are issued with a universal personal identifier (UPI) which is used in all instances on every form and record. Some countries operate this system, but not Britain. It clearly streamlines administrative procedures, but makes information in one area easily accessible in another, and thereby permits swift and comprehensive cross-referencing. The matter of cross-referencing is particularly important in the case of police and medical records.

Police files

It is the computerized records of the police that have caused most concern in Britain. In this connection, it is important to draw a distinction between factual data, such as car registration numbers, and intelligence, which includes hearsay, speculation or the personal observations of police officers. The Police National Computer at Hendon is the centre for a network of around 300 computer terminals which serve police stations throughout the country. The system holds data on millions of people: it holds around 5 million names on the criminal names index; more than 3.5 million sets on the fingerprint file; and is thought to contain 1.23 million files of the Special Branch, 29 000 files from the national immigration intelligence unit, 160 000 from the national drugs intelligence unit, and 67 400 from the Fraud Squad. It also holds over 32 million entries on car owners from the vehicle registration computer at Swansea, and though such data may help the police in preventing crime, it causes concern in that it inevitably includes information on non-criminal persons.

The system can now deal with over 250 000 enquiries a day and, through radio networks, officers anywhere can be given information from national records in a matter of seconds. It is acknowledged that the system includes a considerable amount of suppositional data. According to the Home Office, the Police National Computer is not linked to any other central or local government systems, but Large (1984) claims there is evidence of information being passed between tax authorities, the vehicle registration centre and social security offices. There have also been indications in recent years that associations such as the Anti-Blood Sports League are noted on licence records and it is such developments that protectionists see as infringements of personal liberty.

Expansionists would counter that if a citizen has nothing to hide, then he has nothing to fear. If sophisticated computer systems can assist in more swiftly apprehending criminals, then they are to be welcomed, and without doubt the facilities for storage, swift access and cross-referencing enable the police to provide a far more effective service. This can be most clearly seen in the infamous Yorkshire Ripper case of 1981 where it is now conceded that more effective use of computers would have almost certainly led to an earlier arrest of Peter Sutcliffe. His sixth victim, Jean Jordan, a Manchester prostitute, was paid a freshly minted five pound note by Sutcliffe which was later found in her handbag. Manchester CID contacted their West Riding counterparts and, through the Bank of England, the note was traced to a bank in Shipley and identified as one issued to a number of local employers, including the company where Sutcliffe worked. But though he was interviewed a number of times, the police were satisfied with his story. Much data was being collated on the Ripper, but by different police forces, on different themes, and with manual systems. West Yorkshire police were pursuing other leads, such as the tape-recorded voice, and the various data remained disseminated. It is easy to be wise after the event, but had other information on the Ripper been correlated with the bank note, it would certainly have pointed strongly to Sutcliffe, and a further seven lives could have been saved.

A more advanced system is now being introduced, appropriately named HOLMES (Home Office Large Major Enquiry System), which will store all information that pours into an incident room and give detectives rapid access to it by scanning statements at up to a million words a minute. The system is eventually intended to equip all fifty-one forces with compatible software so that joint investigations can be made more effective. For instance, if a witness recalls seeing a red car, the computer system can provide every other reference to red cars in previous statements; it can combine information from separate investigations; and an officer making inquiries about, say, a blue jumper can also be given references to jerseys, sweaters and pullovers.

Most would welcome such facilities, and in many respects we

already accept various forms of 'technological policing' in our daily lives without particularly taking exception to it. Most of us do not greatly object to speed checks on motorways or TV surveillance in supermarkets. Rooftop cameras are increasingly used for major state occasions and have been introduced at football matches to help combat hooliganism. Digital editing techniques make it possible to bring a face into instant close-up and greatly help in apprehending trouble-makers. At the international level, the development of increasingly swift computer systems assists police forces of different nations in tackling the problems of drug traffic and terrorism.

Nevertheless, pessimists express misgivings. The fear is that different information, much of it possibly impressionistic, can be linked together to provide a totally spurious picture. This can be seen in the case of Jan Martin. Jan applied for a job with a company producing industrial films, but the company was told by one of its major clients that 'she would not be welcome on their premises' because they alleged she had connections 'with terrorists in Europe'. Because Jan's father happened to be a former Detective Chief Superintendent, she was able to establish that the accusation had been leaked from the Special Branch. It appears that while on holiday in Holland she and her husband were in a cafe where the proprietor thought her husband looked like a Bader–Meinhoff terrorist and rang the police. The Dutch police didn't pursue the matter, but the accusation stayed on the file and was relayed to the Metropolitan Police Special Branch.

There is substantial evidence that many employers regard any kind of police record, no matter how innocuous, as a mark against an individual. One American study tested a number of employers with files of job applications containing varying police records, and found that employers were far more likely to employ those with no record at all, even if the record indicated that the individual was later acquitted. Many fear police harassment over perfectly legal activities (e.g. being a member of CND) and suspect that unchecked data can build up to create an 'information mountain' beyond the control of the individual. It is for these reasons that the protectionists are wary of the police use of computers.

Medical records

The second main area of concern after the police is medical records. These do not usually involve as direct a threat to individual liberty, but they clearly contain information of a highly personal and sensitive nature. The situation is similar to the police: the state may wish to create large-scale centralized computer systems for administrative purposes while the medical profession are wary that these intrude on individual privacy. One might say that the DHSS has shown itself to be expansionist while the British Medical Association (BMA) has appeared strongly protectionist. The BMA has, in fact, instructed members not to cooperate with the DHSS's project to computerize health and family details of children from birth on the grounds that the proposed system fails to comply with the BMA's principles over privacy. The BMA are not against computerizing medical records but insist that safeguards should apply and that different forms of information be kept separate. They are not prepared that personal medical records should be interwoven with data held for administrative purposes.

It should not be thought that the requirements of the DHSS and the BMA are necessarily incompatible. With care and imagination, different systems might well be possible with appropriate safeguards, particularly in view of the various forms of hardware now available. In that the Ministry of Health requires detailed, centralized records, these can probably be most effectively held on large mainframe systems, while doctors' practices appear more suited to small-scale integrated micro networks where each doctor could operate a terminal holding patients' records. Such a system is far more effective and secure than the manual system it replaces and releases the doctor from a great deal of administrative work. Those entering data to the system could have personal code numbers, and machines be barred so that different information is available to doctors, nurses and receptionists respectively. If desired, such a system could even be linked to the DHSS system on terms agreeable to all parties. Once again, it is a matter of choice.

Before we leave this discussion we should note that some commentators (who I would term expansionist) believe that during the next half century, the very nature of the problem itself will change, particularly as a result of advances in artificial intelligence. Sir Clive Sinclair, the British microelectronics pioneer, has predicted the emergence of artificial 'super brains' by around 2020 which will take over from the family doctor and other professionals. He forecasts the arrival of meta-computers costing no more than a family car and able to supply all professional knowledge. The machine would know each individual, his or her medical history and personality characteristics and, like the GP, would supply prescriptions, comfort or advice. Likewise, there would be no need to leave home for education or to consult a lawyer. Sinclair believes that in many ways such a system will prove more acceptable, as it will free us from any embarrassment, reduce travelling and provide far greater control over personal records.

Christopher Evans, meantime, envisages equally dramatic changes for the police and optimistically predicts that crime will decline as new information technology makes cash obsolete and more transactions take place electronically. Credit cards become increasingly foolproof as people are issued with personal identity numbers (PINs) and, in future, owners might even be identified through fingerprint patterns. Cable systems, such as QUBE, will provide improved security systems — direct links to police, fire and ambulance — and in Columbus there has already been a marked drop in petty crime. He also predicts fewer motoring offences as people (thanks to electronic communications) have less need to travel; dwindling oil supplies make motoring an extravagance; and the cars that do remain have considerably improved safety and security devices. In short, new technology reduces traditional criminal activity, though Evans acknowledges a possible rise in civil disturbance as society re-adjusts to new circumstances.

Computer crime
Pessimists would respond that Evans underplays the potential the computer provides for fresh forms of anti-social activity. He maintains that systems will become increasingly secure, but evidence suggests that one man's ability to devise new security checks is matched by another's ability to get round them. 'Computer crime' is now big business, and though continuous attempts are made to check the abuse, leakage and dissemination of information, signs are that it will remain a never-ending battle.

Sources suggest losses from computer crime in the United States of up to 5 billion dollars a year, and this is probably an under-estimation as companies are reluctant to admit they are subject to it. Many firms seem reluctant to spend the necessary funds to make their computers secure, and Tapper insists that if they did, the problem would be largely resolved. Banks and other financial institutions seem particularly prone to criminal activity, which can include taking advantage of 'bugs' in systems, stealing software or unofficially altering it. Theft of computer time (e.g. the use of computers by employees for non-work activities) is another growing area though workers rarely regard it as crime. Indeed, it seems that the computer criminal is more likely to be a relatively honest person in a position of trust, which suggests perhaps that the computer provides us with a new type of criminal and changing sets of values. In 1984, two American teenagers, using domestic computers, broke into the Pentagon's secret ARPA computer network; and a year later seven more teenagers tapped into computers across the US, made free international phone calls, and moved telecommunications satellites across space. Criminals or whizz-kids? Examples are endless of people who have penetrated systems, and many would not share Evans' optimism that as technology progresses so criminal behaviour will decline. The situation seems analogous to that of earlier technologies such as the motor car: cars today greatly assist the police to solve crimes, but they also permit a whole range of criminal activities previously unknown.

Data havens

Another important issue is that of trans-border data flow and data havens. Satellite technology has made it possible for data from one country to be processed in another, and many European organizations in the 1970s found that the cheapest way to update their systems was to do this in the United States, at night, when computers were not being used. In the Swedish town of Malmo, for instance, the local fire brigade had an excellent computerized system containing details on all properties, and if a fire broke out they knew in seconds how many men to send, how to equip them, how long the ladders should be, if elderly people were involved etc. The data for this system was updated during 'quiet time' on a system in Ohio, USA, and such services proved highly lucrative, particularly for America.

But this also provided an attractive sanctuary for those organizations wishing to hold data (perhaps of a dubious kind) that was illegal at home. Some states became 'data havens' — refuges for data that was illegal elsewhere — and a good example is Singapore which became a data haven for certain Australian companies. In the 1970s, Britain too gained an unsavoury reputation as one of the last remaining data havens in the developed world, and many countries wished to divorce themselves from such activities, partly because of the implications for their own data-processing employment. Just as pornography, drugs and great train robbers seem to gravitate to those countries with the most lax legislation, the same appeared the case with 'dirty data'.

Nations began to protect themselves by introducing data protection legislation. Sweden was first in 1973, followed by other European states such as Denmark, Norway, Luxembourg, West Germany, France, Holland, Austria, Belgium, Portugal and Spain. These laws vary considerably, but most cover data held on individuals by both public and private bodies, and are legally enforcible. Sweden suspended the Malmo operation as the United States lacked legislation, and the Americans became concerned they might be cut off from European operations. Along with Canada, they too introduced legislation, but it was weaker in that it only applied to the public sector and compliance was voluntary. Other countries such as Australia and New Zealand also passed appropriate legislation.

Britain's response to the data protection issue remained somewhat dilatory, and protectionists became critical of this. As countries began protecting themselves, so they made trans-border flow illegal with those not covered by appropriate legislation, and Britain was in danger of becoming isolated. For instance, an English firm got the contract to produce national health cards for Sweden, but the Swedes withdrew because they were not prepared for their health records to be sent to a 'data haven'. Much of our existing law was simply obsolete for an electronic age. For example, under English law, orders by electronic mail, by satellite, were not proper orders as they were not 'in writing'. Finally, the situation meant that Britain had no effective means of dealing with computer crime, and the FBI in America had calculated that this was rising at a rate of 400 per cent a year.

In 1981 a Council of Europe Data Protection Convention came into operation which in effect created an exclusive club of member states who, having accepted certain principles, would then transfer electronic data between themselves. As Britain became a signatory, this in effect obligated us to introduce legislation. Had we been left out and member states denied data to us, this would have run serious risks for multi-national companies, major banking and financial institutions, and scientific research. Overwhelming support for data protection legislation came from the business community, the trade unions, the computer industry and the professions.

The drafting of a Data Protection Bill in Britain was therefore very much in response to pressure from the international business community. With new technology, the multi-national companies are particularly important for they have played a major role in stimulating trans-national data exchange and have become adept at transferring data much as they wish. A single multi-national may now operate its own communication network serving over 500 computers in, say, 100 cities in twenty different countries. National laws have become increasingly difficult to operate, and if problems arise over the holding of data, companies can store it in one country, process it in another, while manufacturing and selling in others. Such tactics might also be adopted to weaken the power of particular trade unions or work groups, or even to obtain cheaper clerical staff. Information can now be transmitted so swiftly and cheaply that its location is increasingly irrelevant to the function it performs, and Kerr and Bell would no doubt see this as representative of the convergence they identified.

The Data Protection Act, 1984

Parliament passed a Data Protection Act in 1984, though as we have seen (and government ministers admit this) it resulted more from political and commercial pressures than any burning concern over individual privacy. However, it incorporated the important principle of an individual's 'right to know' and in this respect deviated from the earlier Lindop report. Individuals may see data held on them and correct it where necessary, as it should be accurate, kept up to date and only retained as long as needed. Personal information may be obtained, held, processed and distributed, but only for specific purposes, and it should be adequate but not excessive for those purposes. The storage of data for speculative reasons is illegal.

Any users of computer systems containing personal information (including police computers) have to register with a Data Protection Registrar by March 1986, and users must tell the registrar what information is being held, where it comes from and what is its purpose. At the time of writing, the Act only affects commerce and industry, but after 1987 the private citizen will be able to check that personal information held in computer databanks is accurate and only being used for lawful purposes. Any unregistered person storing computerized personal information after that date will be committing a criminal offence, and anyone found using inaccurate information will be liable to pay compensation.

However, there are exemptions, including national security systems, home computer systems, club records, and information held for payroll and accountancy purposes, none of which is covered by the legislation. Lawyers may also be exempt in cases where professional confidentiality could be breached, while examination results are granted limited protection. Finally, individuals are not able to check information relating to tax matters or the prevention or detection of crime (which in practice covers the most sensitive police files), and there are also various discretionary powers vested in the Home Secretary with regard to medical records.

Criticisms

The Act has attracted considerable criticism from protectionists. In the first instance, the BMA and National Council for Civil Liberties (NCCL) have complained that, unlike most other countries, the Act only covers computer records, when 95 per cent of medical records, for example, are still manual. This allows people to simply choose not to computerize in order to stay outside the law. Hewitt (1984), for the NCCL, acknowledges that computers increase the *scale* of the problem but insists that the principle of the citizen's right to know relates every bit as much to manual systems. Dawson (1984), for the BMA, believes there are only around 200 computer systems at present operating among 26 000 doctors in 8000 surgeries (few of which 'talk' to each other) and probably only a dozen major systems running in hospitals. He too laments the exclusion of manual records. The BMA are also uneasy at the considerable discretion granted to the Home Secretary to withhold data appertaining to individuals' medical records. Even the supposedly independent registrar is appointed by the Home Office (and therefore by the political party in power), and under the Police Act doctors are still required to supply data for police purposes. The BMA are concerned over all these issues.

The NCCL is critical of the definition of 'national security' which allows a matter to be so certified if a cabinet minister deems it so. They also criticized the Act for including the registration of computer users, but not computer *systems*. This means that the Home Office, for instance, can register as one user even though it may operate fifteen major national systems of personal data. The form of registration therefore makes it difficult to ascertain precisely what data is being kept. In the case of national security, the NCCL feels that the public should know what files are held, if not their content. Hewitt also criticizes the omission of Lindop's 'codes of conduct' and questions whether the proposed voluntary codes will ever materialize into anything meaningful. Linked to this is the fact that the Data Protection Registrar has fewer powers, a smaller staff and less opportunities for monitoring than the Data Protection Authority envisaged by Lindop. The Conservative government rather saw the DPA as a 'quango' (for which it had a marked distaste) and preferred a simplified scheme that involved the bare minimum necessary to protect personal data. Computer users will only have to abide by the general principles, not any detailed codes of conduct, and there is a Data Protection Tribunal to hear appeals against the registrar's decisions.

Many pessimists question whether the government is seriously committed to data protection legislation and feel that the Bill is 'too little too late'. After the Younger report of 1972 and the even more radical Lindop report of 1978, the Act is seen by many as a pale shadow. In general, critics argue that the limited powers of the registrar, the exclusion of manual records, the system of registration, the lack of detailed codes of conduct and the considerable number of exemptions mean the Act is minimal, weak, insufficient and barely meeting the requirements of the European convention. It was primarily introduced to ease trans-border data flow, is designed to answer the demands of business interests, national governments and multi-national corporations, and far more meets the wishes of the expansionists than the protectionists.

CONCLUSION

This chapter has considered the possible impact of new technology on citizenship, both as regards representative democracy, and the question of personal privacy. In each case the technology poses both opportunities and dangers. As regards democracy, the technology could result in wider and more regular participation, but could equally dissect the electorate and provide tighter surveillance of political expression and personal activities. Similarly in the case of privacy, more accessible data can greatly assist the provision of police, medical and other governmental services, but at the same time lead to data (possibly false) being held and manipulated without the citizen's awareness.

The optimistic view tends to have a *quantitative* emphasis in that it stresses the expansion of data (and new technology) and suggests that this will prove to be to the overall benefit of society. Pessimists, on the other hand, are less concerned with the amount of data and more with its *quality*: their fear is not that we will experience more data so much as that it may be distorted and inaccurate.

There seems no doubt that in future we shall experience more information — the issue is whether this can be both *open* and *protected*. In Britain, the question of freedom of information has become a particularly thorny one and has inevitably become intertwined with the data protection issue. How do we make more information available to citizens, yet at the same time protect personal information from becoming available to others? In a democratic society, citizens demand access to decision-making, but wish to express that right in private. They also demand access to information that is held on them but equally insist this is denied to others. It is this fundamental clash between freedom of access and confidentiality that is so difficult to maintain in a society where new information technology is increasingly prevalent. The central dilemma is this. If society involves more people in decision-making, then their views are more likely to become known to all. Similarly, if it produces more data and makes it accessible to those it concerns, so it invariably makes it more accessible to others as well.

The issues of access and privacy provide us with a 'see-saw' situation for it would appear difficult to improve one without jeopardizing the other. This is not a new problem for democracy, but information technology intensifies it and makes the whole issue of citizenship extremely complex. Pessimists such as the NCCL are eager for personal data to be made more available to citizens, and Cohen (1984), in a study of different kinds of record-keeping systems, argues that opening systems and respecting the rights of individuals actually leads to *better* systems and improved democracy. But clearly, greater openness increases the problems of protection. Interestingly Masuda, an arch-optimist, argues on similar lines and believes that more open access will come about as a result of participatory democracy. This brings together the two themes of this chapter. He argues that by giving citizens participatory rights, we at the same time give them greater access to, and control over, data that is held on them. In his 'citizens' society', new information technology is autonomously controlled by citizens and privacy ceases to be an issue. The problem with this scenario — in which presumably everyone has total access to all information at all times — is that the fundamental democratic right of individual privacy no longer exists at all. Each society must seek a balance between these concerns and introduce appropriate legislative safeguards. New technology does not impose certain measures: this is a matter of choice.

CHAPTER EIGHT

The Home

Just as new technology is invading the factory and office, so it is invading the home. Work and home are not of course separate spheres of activity, for we noted earlier that many may work from home in the future, but here I wish to discuss mainly non-work aspects of life — leisure pastimes, domestic chores, family activities etc. — and how they will be affected by technological change. Again, because of the vast range of applications, I shall focus the debate by concentrating on particular forms of technology.

Technology in the home is of course nothing new. Television, the telephone and the washing machine are obvious examples, but established products will be transformed while other new domestic appliances and facilities will become available. Take the case of television. Not only is the set now infested with chips — for tuning, colour correction, channel selection etc. — but the various graphics one sees on the screen are created by computer, and the major news items that appear 'instantly' from all parts of the world are provided by 'electronic news gathering'. Chips similarly appear in washing machines, microwave ovens, dishwashers, record players, sewing machines etc. Particularly important, the chip can be used to regulate services to the whole home. In the United States, a computer system called Breslin will wake you up; give you the time, weather forecast and your day's appointments; switch on the radio and make you a coffee; act as a burglar alarm; open the garage doors; control all heating, lighting and cooling; address Christmas cards; play *Happy Birthday* once a year; and maintain all financial accounts. Most remarkable of all are the domestic robots that can dust, vacuum, serve drinks, water plants and wash dishes, and the

American RB5X domestic robot will even operate a fire extinguisher at certain temperatures.

Technology can be of particular benefit to the elderly and handicapped at home. In Sweden, the telephone authority, Televerket, has developed an alarm system to which old people's homes are connected. Similar systems operate in the United States and Britain, based on sensors located in apartments, whereby if movement is not registered over a period of 8 hours, an alarm is raised. Elderly residents can wear emergency buttons that they press if they have an accident or become ill. In London, local authorities have introduced hand-held terminals for social workers to ascertain the welfare benefits to which clients are entitled.

Generally speaking, I feel that there is much to be optimistic about regarding new technology in the home. It will remove many domestic chores which even the most dedicated housewife would find difficulty enthusing over; it can increase safety and security; and it should provide extra time and opportunity for more fulfilling family activities. However, pessimists argue that the danger of a Breslin system is that the technology becomes one's master rather than one's servant. Just as working skills are transferred to machines, so the human activities of waking up, ascertaining the weather, remembering commitments, making decisions etc. are taken from us and we cease to think for ourselves. As a result, the routinized work practices of factory and office spill over into the home. Reinecke expresses concern over isolation and loneliness as more people use digitally-controlled washing machines rather than go to the local laundrette, and play computer games on their own rather than bridge with the neighbours. All the electronic leisure activities are concentrated inside the domestic fortress; they do not encourage its occupants to look outside it.

In similar vein, Simons (1985) talks of 'computer phobia' and suggests that the imposition of new technology on people's lives can create states of psychological and emotional anxiety. We become fearful of being outdone by technology in those areas in which we most pride ourselves. Why bother to play chess when a computer can beat you? Why bother to learn maths when an expert system can perform all the calculations you require? Why bother to play the violin when a micro-controlled synthesizer can do it better?

Personally, I find all this a bit strong. In the factory situation, the worker may experience feelings of alienation — be prevented from applying his skills, or compelled because of noise and line speed to work in a state of isolation — but in the home, these effects seem far less apparent, if only for the obvious reason that one is largely one's own boss. There is clearly an element of choice: one does not *have* to use technology to record all one's engagements; and if you prefer playing bridge with the neighbours to computer games, you are free to do so. And surely many enjoy playing chess or the violin even though they know they will never be a Karpov or Menuhin. The debate is similar to the one surrounding television, often branded the 'goggle box' and 'conversation killer'. While it can isolate people in their homes and feed them mindless pap, it can equally stimulate, educate and inform, and as easily serve as a 'conversation maker' when people enquire of each other whether they saw a particular play or news item.

I am therefore not convinced that new technology in the home is automatically a bad thing and, indeed, few have expressed concern at this level of pessimism. The debate has been waged more at lower levels, over how it will be introduced and controlled in capitalist societies such as Britain, and whether it will lead to the enhancement or decline of out-of-work activities. Optimists argue that new technology will 'upgrade' the quality of home life in cultural terms, while pessimists fear it will have a 'downgrading' effect.

This discussion also allows us to focus on other new technologies which so far have only received passing mention; namely, cable and satellite systems. I stressed in the introduction that the full impact of the chip is only felt when it is linked to such technologies, particularly in the field of telecommunications. In this chapter we shall therefore focus upon *communication*, the third strand, along with information and production, of the micro explosion. As a vehicle for this discussion, I shall mainly talk about what is probably the most important, and contentious, piece of technology in the home – television. But before that, a few general words on how homes in Britain have so far responded to new technology.

THE BRITISH RESPONSE

The extent to which British households will adopt new technology is constantly underestimated. Despite our reputation, certainly in the industrial field, for being non-technological, the British home seems fascinated by new forms of equipment and gadgetry. In 1965 the BBC predicted 750 000 colour sets by 1975; ITV, 2 million; in fact there were 8 million. The same can be said of video recorders (an American invention largely manufactured in Japan), where Britain has become the world's best market. More videos are rented or bought in Britain than the USA (with four times our population), and nearly as many as Japan (with twice our population), and one in three homes now has one. Most important of all, Britain has been particularly prominent in the use (and manufacture) of home microcomputers. Home computer sales soared by 400 per cent in 1982 alone, and the UK now has nearly twice as many as Germany, France and Italy combined. (This contrasts with the industrial field where we are behind Germany and only just ahead of France.)

A point to stress, however, is that this personal computing boom invariably involves *one-way* communication. The real gains obtained from home computers is when they are linked with external services in *two-way* communication. To illustrate this, let us return to the QUBE system in Columbus, Ohio, which was introduced in the last chapter (Fig. 8.1).

Columbus was the first American 'wired city', offering thirty channels of cable TV and various two-way communications such as electronic shopping, information services, home security services,

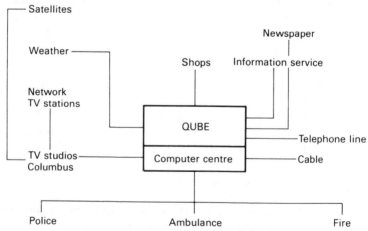

Figure 8.1   The QUBE system, Columbus, Ohio

instant voting etc. People can order goods from shops direct (and have their bank accounts debited automatically); are linked to the police, fire and ambulance services for instant security; and can obtain all kinds of information — newspapers, travel, weather etc. — as well as television shows from home and abroad. Plumbers, doctors and electricians are also being added to the system.

With regard to this form of two-way communication, Britain has been far less successful. Prestel, for instance — a British videotex invention linking subscribers to computerized databanks through telephone lines — has proved disappointing, for sales have been poor. Prestel not only provides vast amounts of data, but allows the subscriber to cross-question the computer down the line, which avoids the hassle of phone delays, paper work etc. usually involved in booking a flight or arranging an overdraft. The central computer also stores programs, and because a home microcomputer has a memory, programs can be transferred to it. Specialized companies now market program packages through Prestel, which provide facilities for architects, lawyers, doctors, accountants, and others working from home. The ordinary householder can also obtain information relating to tax returns, do-it-yourself, conveyancing, or whatever.

But by 1982, 80 per cent of the 16 000 Prestel sets were being used in business — for such services as TOPIC, the stock exchange reports — and only 10–20 per cent were in the home. This makes Reinecke suspicious that Prestel will be controlled by the existing media empires and, far from providing a further tool for democracy, will only meet the interests of business. He also believes the cost will remain prohibitive to most householders for some time to come. By 1985, however, there were over 51 000 Prestel TV sets in use, with 2000 new subscribers arriving every month, and the business/home ratio had narrowed to 55/45. Take-up, therefore, has started to increase though it remains slow overall.

But telephone lines are just one technology that can be linked with computers to provide two-way interactive services. Far more important are cable and satellite, two areas from which Britain has been largely absent. It is these two technologies — often presented as alternatives, but in fact creating their greatest impact when used in conjunction — that will most significantly affect electronic communication to and from the home.

CABLE AND SATELLITE

Cable systems have been available for some time, providing television programmes to people's homes, but have never been widespread in Britain. In 1982, around 14 per cent of the population received TV by cable, compared with 35 per cent in West Germany, 37 per cent in France, 22 per cent in the United States, and over 50 per cent in Belgium, Holland, Denmark and Canada. The government intends (as proposed in the 1982 Hunt report) to rewire the whole of Britain with broadband cable to carry TV, information, telecommunications, video and data. The problem with cable is that it is expensive to install (some claim as high as £6000 million for 60 per cent of Britain), and consequently it is unlikely to reach outlying, rural areas. Its great appeal, particularly with new fibre-optic cabling, can be summarized under three main headings:

- It offers expanded channel capacity
- It offers two-way communication
- It can easily be coupled with other communications technologies

With cable, we can refer to a four-circle strategy. The first and innermost circle is the home, as home networks connect TVs, cookers, washing machines, alarm systems, home computers etc. The second circle is the workplace which can be linked through local area networks (LANs). The third circle is the local/district loop which connects homes, businesses and services in a community network. The fourth circle is the national telephony network. (If we add satellite, we can talk of a fifth, international circle.) This means that cable is about far more than extra channels of television — though this may act as the stimulus — and allows the wired community to be created.

Cabling can be done in one of two ways:

- co-axial — this has been used in the United States, is cheaper, but does not carry as much 'traffic' and therefore is not thought by many the best long-term investment
- fibre-optic — new, expensive, but vastly superior in terms of quality and service provision

This creates something of a dilemma for government. Britain

could develop a world lead in fibre-optic technology (which is unquestionably the superior form of cabling) and gain significant export markets, but the cost may prove off-putting to cable operators (who are primarily interested in offering TV) and the 'cable revolution' may never take place. The Milton Keynes experiment suggests that costs are 25–40 per cent higher and this has made companies hesitant to invest in cable. Consequently, the government is encouraging fibre-optic cabling but *permitting* co-axial. The smaller companies will almost certainly opt for co-axial, but this will only offer up to two dozen channels and a restricted range of two-way services. The NEDC and major electronics companies feel strongly that Britain should adopt fibre-optic cabling because it is getting cheaper; British Telecom are already using the technology for phone links; and Britain could develop a valuable export market. Whatever is installed could be there well into the next century, so the decision is important. We have considerable expertise in fibre-optic cabling, but initial costs are high and it is difficult to ascertain the likely demand for cable services. Once laid, cabling becomes cheaper as 50–100 subscribers can be served from the new, improved 'star' systems, but the difficulty is knowing when, and how much, to invest. We could be advantaged by entering late (as with colour television) but equally find ourselves rapidly falling behind.

In France, a number of projects are being developed, as in Biarritz, where viewers get fifteen TV channels and their telephone through fibre-optic cable. All subscribers to the system TELETEL, are issued with a viewdata machine — a visionphone instead of the traditional phone directory. A directory is always a third out of date at the moment of issue anyway — due to people moving, dying, installing a phone etc. — and though initial costs for visionphones are high, they do not need to be reissued and all information can be constantly updated. The computer base now holds 23 million entries, and 50 000 updates are made every day. The visionphone also incorporates a videotex service for local teleshopping, banking and mail ordering. In 1974, France had just 6 million phone subscribers, but now there are 21 million, and the country is a world leader in telecommunications. Whereas about half the French phone network was computer run by 1985, Britain had only three System X exchanges at work on the national network.

The uncertainty over cable has led some to advocate satellite as a preferable alternative. Its great appeal is its universality: if you want it, you can get it. A satellite system can cover a third of the globe, cross national boundaries, provide anything up to 600 channels, and can be beamed down to anyone anywhere with the appropriate receiver. But costs would again be prohibitive for the domestic user and an enormous number of receiver dishes would be needed to provide TV to all who wanted it. In addition, the cost of a transmitter for interactive services would be considerable, and these will not be developed by satellite alone.

Therefore, it is when satellite and cable are used in conjunction that their importance becomes fully apparent. This can be illustrated by Project Universe, a huge electronic system set up in 1983 involving 150 computers at seven different British sites (Fig. 8.2). The project brought together for the first time different makes of computers (with a variety of functions and using several languages) to study how they could be joined by high-speed digital links. It not only exchanged data, but ran an electronic mail system and allowed designs to be displayed and worked on simultaneously at different sites. The participants were the universities of Cambridge, Loughborough and London, Marconi, Logica, British Telecom Research, and the Science and Engineering Research Centre. At the heart of the project were fifteen local area networks which linked incompatible computers from the seven sites through cable and satellite. Once information left a site, it went to a switching device which re-coded the data into information for the satellite, and an earth station then sent signals 36 000 km to the Orbital Test Satellite (OTS), from where it was sent down to another earth station. The project received considerable international recognition and has led on to further research programmes.

TELEVISION

I shall now consider some of these themes and issues, particularly cable and satellite, in relation to television. In this way we can see why optimists regard these technological incursions into the home as a great boom, while pessimists view them with alarm. Cable and satellite between them can provide a vast range of TV channels from all parts of the world, which will make television more akin to the written word, with people receiving a wide range of communication (instead of a narrow handful of channels) and national

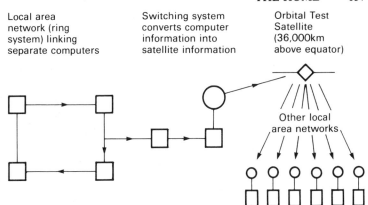

Local area
network (ring
system) linking
separate computers

Switching system
converts computer
information into
satellite information

Orbital Test
Satellite
(36,000km
above equator)

Other local
area networks

Figure 8.2 Project Universe

governments increasingly unable to control/censor material. There
will also be enormous problems of copyright, and just as people
have for years (illegally) recorded material from radio and record
players on to domestic tape recorders, so now television material
(often costing considerable sums to produce) will become available
to all. This will greatly change — both in quantitative and qualitative terms — the style of TV entertainment entering the home and
almost certainly lead to a major restructuring of broadcasting as we
know it in Britain. But, overall, will this be for the better?

The Hunt Committee was asked to consider *how*, not *if*, cable
TV should be introduced, and the main theme of its report was that
operators should not be required to provide a balance of programmed services, but should be free, within the law, to show
whatever material (e.g. foreign programmes, advertising etc.) they
so wished. Pay-as-you-view TV could be introduced, but cable
operators would not be allowed to acquire exclusive rights to major
events, and would have to carry all BBC and IBA programmes
(though not immediately). Most controversial of all, Hunt proposed that operators could show 'X rated material' so long as an
electronic 'locking' device was used to stop children watching it.
One company would have the sole franchise (probably for ten
years) to run the cable system in a particular locality, and would
then sub-contract channels to others who would recruit programme
makers. Cable companies would therefore offer three main services:

(a) BBC and IBA television and radio; (b) interactive services; (c) cable channels.

Such proposals are termed 'deregulation' in that there is a move away from centrally (and often publicly) controlled broadcasting authorities to local, privately owned companies, such as has occurred in the United States. It is important to stress, however, that there are two forms of deregulation in broadcasting: of access and of content. The Hunt report was generally recognized as a liberal, strongly deregulating document in both senses of the word. Hunt was anxious that control of cable TV should be spread as widely as possible and that companies be granted maximum freedom with regard to content. Technological developments made it nonsense to do otherwise. Thus companies would be free to show foreign imports, adverts, pornography, violence etc., within minimal constraints, for this was the way in which business would be generated and cable systems expanded.

The following year the government issued a white paper which endorsed many of Hunt's proposals, but laid greater stress on the control of cable companies, the amount of imported material, and standards of taste and decency. In short, it was somewhat less deregulatory in terms of access, and considerably so with regard to content.

The main points of the white paper can be summarized as follows:

- Franchises of twelve years' duration would be offered to companies prepared to use co-axial cabling, and twenty years to those prepared to use fibre-optic cabling. Star networks had to be used with either form of cabling.
- Pay-per-view would be permissible, allowing people to pay for viewing certain items.
- Restrictions are imposed on imported material.
- Taste and decency rules will be the same for cable as for current TV: cable channels will be subject to the Obscene Publications Act.
- Cable advertising would be held to ITV levels, but channels devoted to classified advertising would be permitted. Programme sponsorship would also be allowed.
- Experiments in Milton Keynes (Britain's only 'wired' town) would be extended swiftly to at least ten other towns.

- The Cable Authority should exercise a 'light touch' and intervene as little as possible. Prior submission of programme schedules should not be necessary. Operators would have to carry existing BBC and IBA TV and radio services and any forthcoming satellite services.
- Cable providers and operators must be companies under UK or EEC control.

There would therefore be three tiers of cable operators:

(a) The cable owners — who own the actual cable link.
(b) The cable operators — who obtain the rights to sell and operate a package of TV channels along the cable.
(c) The programme makers — who make and provide programmes to the operators.

In different parts of the country (or even in different parts of a city), these could be closely interwoven or totally separate entities.

This policy will prove a tricky one to follow. For instance, government may insist that cable companies carry BBC and ITV programmes, but if cable operators are to be attracted, these are the very conditions they will want to see removed. Access and content are therefore inextricably intertwined in privately owned media operations — as can be seen in the case of the press — and the practicality of such a policy remains to be seen.

In a 1982 report, the Information Technology Advisory Panel (ITAP) — the six-man advisory team to the Prime Minister — envisaged Britain beating the rest of Europe in a market-driven, private enterprise re-wiring for multi-choice cable TV and interactive electronic services by 1985. It simply didn't happen. Kenneth Baker had forecast thirty channels of cable TV for over half the homes of Britain, but in fact there were none. In a further 1985 report (which has remained unpublished), ITAP insisted that local cable networks must still, and will, be built and that TV will be the drawing force, but the £2.5 billion needed for cabling Britain would not just come from market forces: the government had to become more involved, as in other European countries. Many British viewers have been attracted to home video for feature films, while others appear to retain a loyalty to the BBC and ITV; all of which makes it difficult for cable to become established without government assistance.

The present expectation is that cabling will expand from 400 000 homes in 1985 to 4 million by 1990, but the climate remains highly uncertain. In 1983 the government announced the first eleven franchises, but to date Swindon is the only one offering a multi-channel service. It costs £200 to cable a house, and though 3500 can obtain the service, only 10 per cent subscribed in the first year. This means that it will take Swindon cable three to four years to make any money, and even then it may well not survive. In 1985, Croydon Cable Television began laying cable to 16 000 homes to make it the biggest pilot scheme to date, and operations are starting in Aberdeen, Coventry and Westminster. But serious problems remain with other franchises and overall take-up remains slow. The much talked of switched-star technology is not available, and many do not see interactive services before the turn of the century.

Cable illustrates well the point we have made throughout — that because a technology has a certain capability, it does not necessarily mean it will be adopted. Evans may describe a world in which everyone uses interactive services, but political decisions will determine if and how they are introduced into different countries. In Britain, the government's strategy has been to develop cable through the private sector (in contrast to France) by encouraging companies to provide a wider range of broadcasting facilities. The policy is therefore 'entertainment-led': this will provide the stimulus to develop a cable infrastructure, and once this is laid, the interactive services will follow. But the strategy has clearly run into trouble, for cable companies are deterred by the high cost of fibre-optic cabling; are reluctant to carry BBC and IBA programmes which the government are wanting to protect; and were hit by the Chancellor's removal of 100 per cent allowances on capital expenditure in the 1984 budget.

Even if cable television does become established, there are still doubts as to whether this will lead to the development of interactive services. In the first place, they will be restricted if cable companies (as seems likely) go for co-axial cabling but, more important, there are indications that those who are attracted to cable television have little interest in two-way services. A 1985 study by JICCAR (the joint body representing both cable industry interests and the advertisers) suggested that the average cable TV viewer is likely to be a low-skilled manual worker, with a larger than average family, living on an urban council estate, who expects all the family (from

18 months upwards) to be avid TV viewers at all times of the day. But he has little interest in two-way services. Hence the paradox: those with cable are least likely to use it for interactive services; those who might develop such services do not receive cable.

As regards satellite, the situation is not dissimilar. By international convention, Britain is allotted a position in space and a set of wavebands to run five DBS (direct broadcasting by satellite) channels targeted at the British Isles. In 1981 the BBC was offered the first two, and in 1983 the IBA were offered channels 3 and 4, but because of high costs a consortium was formed in 1984 — the so-called 21 Club — which included the fifteen ITV companies, the BBC and five independent groups. In 1985, however, the whole scheme was dropped, as the government's insistence on British equipment apparently made the plan uneconomic. Any projects now seem likely to be cheaper and smaller scale, involving lower-powered satellites, and could come from the ITV companies or other commercial concerns.

All this is in sharp contrast to France, where the approach is to see cable, satellite and other forms of telecommunications as public utilities. The wired society is being created by the state, not private entrepreneurs, which is leading to very different kinds of applications and services. The situation is not dissimilar to types of technology discussed earlier such as robotics and word processing. Cable and satellite may appear indispensable technologies for the future, but their arrival — for historical, economic, political and cultural reasons — may take far longer in one country than another. This appears the case in Britain.

The third age of broadcasting

We are entering what might be termed the 'third age of broadcasting' — from radio, to television, to satellite and cable channels. This will involve not merely a revolution in a technological sense, but also in terms of deregulation. The United States indicates the direction in which things are likely to go.

The USA has witnessed a surge of cable TV companies, many of which have made heavy incursions into network audiences. The most successful — such as HBO which runs feature films 24 hours a day — tend to concentrate on news, feature films and sport, or on material (e.g. pornography) not offered on the networks. Many have ceased to remain viable, however (e.g. CBS's cultural channel had to close in 1982), and it seems likely that the market will eventually be dominated by around a dozen companies. This may not even include the three major networks — CBS, NBC and ABC — and by the turn of the century they too could cease to exist.

In this uncertain market, it is interesting that the lead in cable development has been taken, not by the traditional broadcasting organizations, but by proprietors in other branches of the media, such as the press. In 1984, Robert Maxwell entered the UK cable scene in a big way with the purchase of Rediffusion's ready-made, four-channel cable network, covering 1.2 million British homes. This allowed Maxwell to provide pay-television under licence to 700 000 homes in fifty-three towns and, of these, thirty-one (covering 400 000 homes) have been converted to carry other major subscription channels. The purchase was made at a time when confidence in cable was rock-bottom, and under the deal Maxwell also took over the 15-year franchise to put in a cable network serving 20 000 homes in Guildford; a cable television development centre at Coombe in Surrey; and a 14 per cent stake in a feature film cable television channel, United Cable Programmes.

Meanwhile, Maxwell's erstwhile newspaper rival Rupert Murdoch has also been expanding in the television field with the launch of his Sky satellite channel, operating from a small London studio, sending out pop videos, sport, comedies etc. to viewers as far apart as Finland and Tunisia. It has yet to make a significant impact in Britain, but has proved particularly popular in Holland where it has 3 million subscribers. This is no doubt due to the fact that the 14 million Dutch audience is already considerably fragmented — between two Dutch, three German and a Belgian channel — and is attracted by the addition of a commercial, English-speaking station. A similar venture, being run by a group of American businessmen working from Luxembourg, is Coronet, which eventually hopes to carry sixteen channels into every European country.

In 1985, Twentieth Century Fox (the film studio which Murdoch owns) merged with Metromedia, the largest chain of TV stations in the United States, to give Murdoch partial control of stations in seven key American cities. These reach nearly 20 per cent of US homes, and the deal puts him in the forefront of the American TV industry with the potential to challenge the big three networks. The price he has to pay is taking out American citizenship, for the rules of the Federal Communications Commission forbid foreigners to own more than 20 per cent of a US TV station. They also require that no one can own a TV station and a newspaper in a single city and, though he is in the clear in Washington, Houston, Dallas and Los Angeles, he may have to sell the *New York Post* and *Chicago Sun-Times*, unless he can find a way round the regulation. On the Australian side, the price is the surrender of his Australian TV stations in Sydney and Melbourne, for the Australian Broadcasting Tribunal requires all station owners to be Australian. Speculation is that he may restructure his company, News Ltd, or sell the stations to his mother to circumvent the law and enable him to retain his interest. These kinds of developments are fast making national broadcasting boundaries, network structures and even legal requirements increasingly obsolete. No doubt Kerr and Bell would again argue they support the convergence thesis.

The upgrading view
There are optimists who welcome these developments and believe they will enhance and upgrade the quality of home entertainment. They maintain that television provides a rich source of varied material and that if people now have a larger choice this is all to the good. They feel that in Britain especially — with our long tradition of public service broadcasting through the BBC — we have for too long fostered an elitist, exclusive view of broadcasting, and that this should be removed. The emergence of independent television (so fiercely resisted in 1954) is now generally accepted as having provided a healthy air of competition, and the additional BBC and ITV channels have catered for minority interests, some of which (thanks to television) have become major events (e.g. snooker). Educational facilities such as the Open University and the BBC Microcomputer programme have been universally acclaimed, and the growth of cable and satellite merely allows this kind of provision to be further extended. A wider range of channels allows people to watch what they want to see, not what network programme controllers decide is good for them, and this removes much of the stuffiness from British broadcasting. Optimists argue that this can only be welcomed in democratic society. It should also, given the wide choice available, make people more selective in their viewing and less inclined to sit in front of the set gaping at whatever happens to be on.

Many also see cable as an opportunity for entrepreneurship,

export sales and general economic expansion. Various politicians and proprietors, such as Murdoch and Maxwell, take this line, and many independent producers welcome release from the paternalism of the BBC and IBA. Leading names from British entertainment (e.g. Peter Bowles, Jonathan Lynn, David Puttnam, Michael Peacock etc.) have welcomed the government's pay-per-view proposals on the grounds that it will encourage British programme makers, for people will pay to watch new British material (rather than old movies) but will not pay for a whole *channel* (as proposed by Hunt) of minority British interest programmes. The argument is that this will raise bidding prices for special events and bring the maximum amount of revenue to cable. The greater number of channels, coupled with the fall in technology and production costs, should lead to more low-cost, high-quality programmes.

In the United States, Ted Turner, the cable magnate who runs the WTBS station in Atlanta, believes new developments in telecommunications will help 're-industrialize' America. His CNN (Cable Network News) channel already has 35 million US subscribers and in 1983, when TV AM came on the air in Britain, Turner offered his satellite news service to the independent company, free of charge, but the Post Office refused to put a receiver dish on the Camden Lock roof. The service is now available in seventeen countries, and Turner eventually hopes to reach 200.

This has caused some consternation (e.g. in the Soviet Union and Eastern Europe), for satellites can be used to spread political propaganda across national boundaries, but optimists see this as a positive, democratizing development which allows citizens of every country to obtain a broader perspective on world affairs and not just the one determined by their national government. Many multinational companies also welcome the opportunity to advertise their products over whole continents, particularly in Europe, which does not have a tradition of television advertising. Finally, others are simply excited by the new technology itself and welcome the opportunity it provides for new forms of broadcasting (e.g. involving viewer participation).

The downgrading view
Pessimists believe that the dangers from cable and satellite broadcasting are considerable, particularly in Britain which has built up a strong international reputation for high broadcasting standards.

The response to those who advocate minimum regulation in broadcasting affairs is that some level of control must always exist (e.g. in deciding over air waves) and that certain forms of regulation may be no bad thing. The public service tradition, it is argued, has produced some commendable features in that it can provide a 'national consensus' in times of crisis, emphasizing unity rather than division; high quality, 'impartial' current affairs reporting; high-calibre artistic, educational and cultural programmes; and special interest programmes for 'sizeable minorities'.

In broad terms, the fear over cable and satellite is that public service broadcasting will be replaced by 'private profit narrowcasting'. Far from providing greater diversity, each channel (on limited resources) will aim to capture the largest possible slice of the audience by showing those programmes (e.g. soap operas, quiz shows, westerns etc.) with the widest possible appeal. Far from broadening choice and encouraging minority interest output, this is likely to result in the re-running of old (and thereby cheap) glossy American imports. The argument is that rather than widening and developing tastes and interest, cable leads to the reinforcement of *existing* tastes; for taking risks and offering surprises are discouraged. The situation becomes akin to that operating in many American cities at present where one has a 'choice' between numerous channels all showing soap operas or chat shows at the same time in the hope of attracting a particular audience.

The concerns of the pessimists can be summarized as follows. First there is a fear of fragmentation: that cable will break up any semblance of a national audience as wealthy cable companies 'buy out' big events (e.g. the Cup Final) and deny accessibility to others. The BBC and IBA oppose pay-as-you-view proposals on these grounds because, although the government insist that 'national events' will be open to all, they are wary as to how these will be defined, especially as the power of cable companies continues to grow.

Linked with this is the insistence that 'self-regulation' is unacceptable in a situation dominated by commercial interests. Ownership is highly concentrated within the media industries, and signs are that satellite and cable will intensify this. The Association of Cinematograph, Television and Allied Technicians (ACTT) saw Hunt as a get-rich-quick recipe for the cable buccaneers and their financial backers, and similarly with the white paper, they felt the government's proposals gave too much power to commercial interests, and believed technical, cultural and employment prospects could suffer. Hood (1984) fears that the owners of cable and satellite systems will inevitably control the message their systems transmit, and argues that these should rather meet social needs and be part of a public communications system.

A third concern relates to cultural identities and the fear that far from creating greater diversity and preserving regional distinctiveness, cable and satellite will smother the world with the same bland (i.e. American) cultural influences. Such fears have been expressed over Sky in Holland, and in France, where Coronet has been labelled the 'coca-cola' satellite. The French are particularly sensitive as they wish to preserve a linguistic identity and are great defenders of public broadcasting. In response, they have launched their own French-speaking satellite, TV5 (carrying no advertising and financed through sponsorship), which has attracted sizeable audiences in France, Belgium and Switzerland, and can now be received in Swindon. They also plan a further four-channel satellite station, Canal 1, which could eventually reach 400 million in over thirty countries by 1986.

A similar situation has arisen in Scandinavia, where home output — with its commitment to national and Nordic identities — has been caught flat-footed by the advent of satellite. The Scandinavian countries planned to beam domestic programmes to each other with Nordsat, but this was torpedoed in 1982 when Denmark withdrew (for fear their language would be eroded), and in 1985 Finland and Norway pulled out of Sweden's proposed Tele-X satellite system. The collapse of Tele-X makes each small nation even more prone to the commercial and cultural pressures exerted by the multi-national companies. Channels like Sky are attractive because most Scandinavians can speak English, and Finland is the only country with any history of TV advertising.

We are faced with a clash between two freedoms: the free flow of information across national borders, and the right of every people to preserve its national and cultural identity. The convergence writers are apt to overstate the gains from the first at the expense of the second, for they suggest that national cultural differences will fade (thanks to world-wide telecommunications) as societies converge towards common values. But true convergence does not occur simply because the whole world is watching *Dallas*! America should be equally prepared to watch television from all other countries and this, of course, does not happen. We have not experienced convergence, but domination — American domination — and many Afro-Asian countries find it impossible, both economically and politically, to develop home-based productions in the wake of cheap, glossy US imports. A 1956 edition of *I Love Lucy* is far cheaper (and often more appealing) than a documentary on local farming methods, and even 14 per cent of British television now consists of American programmes.

A fourth concern relates to regional and social provision. New technology will prove far more economic in the large urban areas, and these could come to receive superior provision. The public service tradition has always stressed an adequate service for all — 'the best of everything for everyone', to quote Lord Reith — but cable is likely to represent an 'urban culture' to the 60 per cent of the population able to receive it. The BBC fear that cable could prove socially divisive and have called for the government to lay down and manage a nationwide cable network. Satellite, of course, could reach all areas but, as we noted, high costs make adoption unlikely.

A fifth area of concern is over trans-border transmission and the possible use of cheaper, low-power satellites to issue propaganda, pornography and violence, and poach good-quality, expensive and successful programmes. To pessimists, the whole area becomes ripe for piracy and political intrusion, and consequently they insist on minimal levels of national and international regulation, not to inhibit and curtail, but to provide a framework within which reputable and creative programme makers can operate. Otherwise a state of 'broadcasting anarchy' could ensue in which propaganda, 'video nasties' and pornography will dominate the cable and satellite channels at the expense of 'quality' productions in drama, music and current affairs.

And, finally, there is fear regarding the British tradition of public service broadcasting, for the BBC and ITV could now be pushed to the margins. The BBC, if it only received a small percentage of the viewing audience, would have difficulty justifying its licence fee, while ITV would find it far harder to attract advertising. With reduced funds, both would be pushed into producing 'instant' programmes — news, sport etc. — rather than major documentary and drama series which take some time to 'mature'. Standards will fall if revenue sources are affected and funds transferred to satellites.

In 1985 the Peacock Committee was set up to investigate the possibility of the BBC taking advertising, but many (especially on the political left) would oppose this. The very series for which British television is best known — *Jewel in the Crown*, *Life on Earth* etc. — would become threatened with extinction, and both the BBC and IBA have expressed concern at this. The so-called 'public access' cable programmes, advocated as a way of providing wider public participation, are dismissed as cheap ways of filling air time with astrologers, job opportunities, house sales and music videos. The pessimists believe that broadcasting should lead as well as reflect, and fear a severe fall in programme standards.

Linked with this is the fear that as broadcasting becomes more entwined with commercial interests and increasing convergence takes place between different forms of new information technology, so governments will feel more able to intervene in areas from which they have traditionally detached themselves. Until recently, politicians rarely mentioned 'broadcasting policy' for this was left in the hands of the 'independent' professional broadcasters of the BBC and IBA. But with government increasingly engaged in the commercial and industrial aspects of information technology, so they have entered the territory of programme planning, as was seen in 1985 when the Home Secretary requested the BBC governors to ban the *Real Lives* programme on Northern Ireland.

CONCLUSION

The introduction of satellite and cable allows for greater diversity of information, education and ideas, but also mass propaganda, violence and puerile entertainment. Will the proliferation of choice lead to healthy democratic pluralism, or a fragmented society increasingly subject to multi-national influences? Will more air time be given to minority interests, or will power simply remain where it is, with the multi-nationals, the media magnates and the United States? Is any form of international control for broadcasting advisable or even feasible? These are the sorts of questions we have raised in this chapter, and once again the outcome is largely a matter of choice. We could have cheap, locally-based TV systems offering a community service for far wider communication and information-sharing; conversely, under the cover of talk about choice and competition, a handful of companies and individuals could penetrate our lives more deeply than ever before. Opinions differ as to the likely outcome and whether it will prove beneficial, but in focusing on television we have been able to consider the crucial technologies of cable and satellite which, linked with microelectronics, will markedly affect both work and the home. The debate surrounding television largely centres on whether one believes it should provide people with what they want, or whether it has a role in cultivating tastes and interests: whether it should reflect or lead. The British tradition — stemming from the BBC's first Director General, Lord Reith — has been that broadcasting should 'inform, educate and entertain'. Reith believed that the function of broadcasting was primarily educative — to train 'character' — and was not there to provide people with what they wanted, for they didn't always know what they wanted. Television's task is therefore to cultivate audiences as well as cater for them, and to introduce people to new interests and views of which they may be unaware. Supporters of this tradition fear that as a result of cable and satellite, standards could fall and television become clogged with mindless trivia catering for the lowest common denominator.

It is interesting that the main criticism of each side against the other is the same; namely, that of authoritarianism. The optimists see the Reithian view as conservative, arrogant, pompous and elitist. It presumes a homogeneous, 'middle-class' national culture which does not exist, and prevents market forces discovering what people demand from a broadcasting system. They also argue that these fears have never been confirmed in other branches of the media: commercial radio has not destroyed Radio 3; the *Sun* has not eliminated *The Times*; and sales of gangster novels do not appear to have adversely affected the sales or status of Dickens. Opening up the air waves allows for 'public broadcasting' in a far truer sense — what we might term 'community broadcasting' — in that the public participate to a much greater extent than was ever permissible under the traditional, centralized broadcasting authorities.

The pessimists, on the other hand, maintain that deregulation permits a far more insidious form of control — that of commercial interests — in which any form of public accountability for broadcasting standards is lost. Reith may have been authoritarian, but at least as head of a public corporation he was answerable to the nation. This brings us back to the recurring theme of invention and innovation and the pessimists' emphasis on the latter. Their concern is not with the technology itself so much as with the way it is introduced and controlled. The key innovators in cable and satellite — Turner, Murdoch, Maxwell etc. — are in no sense technologists, and probably haven't the first idea how a satellite works, but are practical businessmen, media entrepreneurs, who possess the vision, cunning and confidence to apply the new forms of technology. As in the early days of telegraphy and broadcasting, the innovators come from outside the mainstream of communications technology. The three entrepreneurs discussed in this chapter have much in common — few early advantages, international outlook, astonishing energy and determination etc. — and apart from being similarly accused of authoritarianism, seem a million miles away from John Reith, the dour Scottish Presbyterian, who believed the BBC's mission was to provide a public service of excellence. The present-day magnates no doubt see their task as meeting people's wishes, and dislike distinctions between 'high' and 'low' culture. Rupert Murdoch owns both *The Times* and the *Sun*, but does not consider one better than the other; merely different. The signs are that British broadcasting will gradually approximate to the American pattern, with an advertiser-financed sector for mass audiences, minority interest pay-television, and a third sector financed by either private or public subsidy.

My own feelings about new technology in the home are somewhat mixed. I take a fairly optimistic stance towards the improved washing machines and domestic robots for they remove much of the drudgery of housework, provide considerable advantages for the housebound and handicapped and, most important, will remain under the control of the human operating it. This *could* also be said for cable, and hopefully remains the aim of those who wish to introduce the various interactive services. But one is left pondering whether it will ever happen and fearful that the introduction of cable will merely result in downgrading effects on television broadcasting. Commercial interests who seek financial gain from cable and satellite television seem unlikely to assist the development of other facilities or to offer TV as a community service. One is reminded of the fact that, at the start of the industrial revolution, the British ruling classes taught the working people to read, but not to write. This allowed them to read instructions, and the Bible for moral improvement, but did not permit them to answer back. The same could happen with cable.

CHAPTER NINE

A New Work Ethic?

We noted in Chapter 3 that pessimists such as Jenkins and Sherman, and optimists such as Stonier and Baker, all agreed on one thing — that in future, people will spend less time 'at work' (i.e. in employment) than they do at present. Life at work and in the home, and the balance between the two, could change so dramatically that the way we presently think of work and non-work could cease to have any real meaning. It is this broader question, of our whole attitude to work and leisure, that I wish to consider in this chapter.

It is important to remember that work ideologies — by which we mean the collection of values, attitudes, beliefs and opinions that people hold towards work — have not remained static throughout history. The ancient Greeks believed that work brutalized the mind (which is why slaves were used) while the Hebrews saw it as drudgery, a punishment for original sin. With early Catholicism, work became a natural right and duty, but was still subordinate to prayer and contemplation; only with the coming of Protestantism, the effects of which have been felt in the last few centuries, did we develop the attitude to work that we know today. It was Luther, and particularly Calvin, who stressed that work was natural and commendable, and idleness a sin. It was their teaching that elevated the virtues of hard work, thrift and sobriety, and provided the 'industrial work ethic'.

There is therefore nothing 'natural' about work as we know it. Man does not have to work five days a week from nine to five, forty-eight weeks a year or whatever, and when people talk of the 'problem of increasing leisure', this would in fact be nothing new for Western society. In the thirteenth century, a feudal peasant worked around 190 days a year, and it was only with the coming of industrialization that men, women and children came to work appallingly long hours in mills, factories and mines. The modern worker enjoys about 1200 hours per year more free time than did his counterpart in 1890 when the average working week was 62 hours compared with the 40 hours we know today. In terms of the total life span, we should also remember that workers now enter the labour market later and live longer and, in total, experience considerably more non-work time. During the last century we have seen shorter working weeks, longer holidays, earlier retirement etc. which, if anything, is a return to the working patterns of pre-industrial society.

It is also in the industrial age that most people's work has taken the form of 'jobs', and this too may now be coming to an end. Employment became widespread when the enclosures of the seventeenth and eighteenth centuries made many dependent on paid work by depriving them of the use of land and the opportunity to provide a living for themselves. The factory system then destroyed cottage industries and removed work from people's homes, while improvements in transport made it possible for people to commute long distances to work. This particularly put women at a disadvantage: whereas in pre-industrial times, men and women shared productive work in the household and village community, it now became customary for the husband to pursue employment while the unpaid work of home and family was left to the wife. Therefore the present increase in women at work can also be seen as a return to former work patterns.

WORK AND NON-WORK

How is work defined? Many see an element of compulsion in work roles — something you have to do — and also an aspect of payment, but the dividing line is thin (e.g. one may feel compelled to paint one's house in non-work time, but do it oneself in order to save money: it is hard to say whether this is work or leisure). We need to distinguish between activity, which we enjoy doing, and labour, which is work done for someone else to earn a living. As we shall see, new information technology makes these dividing lines increasingly blurred.

In a useful model, Parker (1983) identifies the different com-

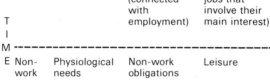

Figure 9.1 Components of life space

ponents of 'life space', by which he means all the activities or ways of spending time that people possess (Fig. 9.1).

The model divides the total amount of time available between work and non-work activities, and suggests that some of these approximate to things we 'have to do' (constraint) and others to things we 'choose to do' (freedom); other activities fall somewhere in between (i.e. various obligations). Work refers to working time, sold time, subsistence time — time spent earning a living — but for some this may contain elements of 'leisure' in that they are doing jobs that involve their main interest (e.g. the actor, sportsman or business tycoon). For such people there is no sharp divide between work and leisure — they are often workaholics — and their work is what they would choose to do with their time anyway. Similarly in non-work activities some time is spent on things we have to do (e.g. eating, sleeping etc.) while pure leisure includes things we choose to do. Between the extremes of constraint and freedom, much time is now spent on activities we feel *obliged* to undertake, in connection with both work and non-work. For instance, many spend considerable time commuting to work: this may involve leisure aspects (e.g. reading a paper, listening to the radio, having a chat etc.) but one would not make the journey unless one was obliged to go to work. Similarly at home, more time is now spent gardening, taking the dog for a walk, picking the children up from school, DIY etc.: for some these may be chores while to others they are important interests, but they cannot easily be classed as work or leisure. They are not things we have to do (or conversely choose to do) in a strict sense, and consequently are best termed 'non-work obligations'.

Of course, some of these activities may overlap (e.g. eating a meal meets a physiological need but may also be a leisure activity), and people fit on to Parker's grid in various ways. Life for a prisoner or the unemployed is far more constricted in both time and activity dimensions, while for the housewife there is considerable blurring between work, leisure and obligations (which perhaps helps explain why so many find it unsatisfying). Meantime, the 'idle rich', and those doing jobs involving their main life interest, spend far more time towards the freedom end of the continuum. The question is whether new technology will provide similar opportunities for the rest of the population.

NEW INFORMATION TECHNOLOGY AND LEISURE

Parker also examines how new information technology could affect leisure patterns and suggests there are two main aspects to consider. In the first place, new technology will continue to directly influence leisure activities as we saw in the last chapter. Just as leisure has been transformed by technologies such as the car and television, so this will continue with home videos, program libraries, wider travel etc. That leisure will continue to be 'technologized' is therefore not in serious dispute. What is contentious is whether such changes will lead to more 'creativity', an upgrading or downgrading of leisure activities. This, of course, is highly subjective, for what is creative to one person may not be so to another, but it raises a similar discussion to the one on television in the previous chapter.

Optimists believe that the release of people from the necessities of employment will enable them to pursue qualitatively superior leisure activities. Martin (1978) predicts that a small proportion of the future leisured class will become far more creative, and draws a parallel with the wealthy, non-employed class of Victorian England who produced many of the great inventors, writers and musicians. Leisure will increasingly provide greater freedom for individual choice and expression; people will not just passively accept the provisions of mass entertainment. Individuals will instead manipulate and exploit them; accepting some, rejecting some, and modifying others. Fifth-generation machines, by making complex techniques available in simplified form, will spawn a new kind of 'renaissance man' — able to obtain a deep knowledge of science, literature, music etc. — and with increased leisure time people will be more able to 'work' on activities of their choice.

Pessimists, however, such as those of a Marxist persuasion, have long argued that leisure time will not suddenly become meaningful to industrial workers simply because there is more of it, if the nature of their work degrades them as human beings. They maintain that it is hard for a five-day slave to suddenly feel free at weekends, for stultifying work leads to stultifying leisure, and if people spend most of their time pulling machine handles on assembly lines it is little surprise if they then spend their leisure time playing one-armed bandits in amusement arcades. So long as capitalist society survives and the nature of work continues to be deskilled in the ways suggested in Chapters 4–6, extra non-work time will not necessarily result in an upgrading of leisure activities.

Optimists reject this as a rather elitist view of leisure and argue from a historical viewpoint that working-class culture is qualitatively higher today than it was a century ago. Even if we regard Bingo and the *Sun* as hardly representing 'high culture', both require basic numeracy and literacy which back in Victorian times most of the population simply did not possess. The implication that at that time the population (or even the middle classes) were all immersed in a high culture of theatre, opera etc. is dismissed as a romanticized view. Optimists reject the idea that with increasing leisure, man becomes bored and restless, and even a restless spirit may prove an asset, driving him towards as yet undiscovered interests. They perceive a broadening and enrichening of leisure activities which will extend further as a result of new information technology.

We again see a divide between optimists and pessimists, though each camp agrees that as a result of micro-technology we can expect reductions in working hours which will profoundly affect the work–leisure relationship. My personal hope is that any inability to cope with increased leisure will only prove a transitional problem and that it will increasingly take on the character of work. If one accepts (as I would) that man is naturally energetic, inquisitive, imaginative and creative then, if less time is spent in formal employment, more leisure time will be spent on 'chosen work'. Work and leisure become ever more blurred and fade into what is better termed 'activity', for if our mental balance is not to become totally distorted, then we cannot spend all our new-found leisure time in rest and relaxation. We must discover 'activated' leisure, which could result in a division between

(a) a basic economy in which people work on producing goods and services, and
(b) a secondary economy, in which people work on tasks of their own choosing.

Toffler envisages paid work being done in the basic economy for a minimum time with maximum technology, and 'prosuming' — self-directed work in which goods and services are produced for one's own use — in the secondary economy.

All this affects the time–space model (Fig. 9.1) introduced earlier, for less time is now spent in employment, and work obligations become compressed as more people work from home. While pessimists would argue that time at work is increasingly deskilled, there is some hope that with more leisure time available (and technology providing our basic needs) activities towards the freedom end of the continuum may grow. These could well take the form of non-work obligations and lead to a richer life within the home and family.

A NEW WORK ETHIC?

The Western industrialized world thus becomes faced with a curious paradox. For centuries we have lamented the dehumanizing effects of many forms of work, and sought to reduce toil and improve the quality of working life, but now as we approach the opportunity to perhaps do just this — to live to work instead of working to live — we find ourselves so totally immersed in the protestant work ethic that we are unable to let go of entrenched attitudes and embrace new-found freedoms. Rather like the prisoner who wants to be free but is fearful of the world outside, we are frightened, even if we dislike work, to face a world without it. We welcome the thought of more leisure but at the same time fear that unemployment could threaten the whole fabric of our society. Increased leisure and unemployment can easily become the same thing unless we are careful. Measures need to be taken to ensure the benefits of the former without the tragic consequences of the latter.

It is not simply an economic question. People do not work just to get paid, but to pursue activities with and for others. Work is of crucial importance to individuals in a world that tells them work is commendable, and it is no substitute to pay them to do nothing. It is hard to see enforced leisure ever becoming an acceptable substitute for work, and we have to devise means for

(a) sharing available work, and
(b) inculcating leisure with work-related activities.

This way — by creating a society in which people are no longer primarily paid (or judged) by employment — seems to offer, in the long term, the best hope of avoiding societal breakdown.

The work ethic may therefore be replaced by a 'leisure ethic' in which leisure becomes the central activity in life, with work as a means to that end. Jenkins and Sherman (1981) prefer a 'usefulness ethic' in which work is not abolished, but its creative functions are enhanced by greater choice. Similarly, Clarke (1982) suggests a 'contribution ethic' which recognizes more unpaid work and the things people do for each other.

The most important development, however, could be a move away from labels altogether, and any one over-arching ideology, towards a situation in which individual differences are increasingly recognized. We may experience a number of *competing* ideologies, none of which is totally dominant, and move to a situation in which work ceases to be 'good' and idleness 'bad'. People clearly vary in their needs for work and leisure, and we could experience a society where those who wish to work may do so, while those who do not can be idle (like the ancient Greeks) with a clear conscience. In pre-industrial society work, play and jollification went side by side, and perhaps today we spend too little time helping each other enjoy life. Is the idea that 'work is good for you' and must be pursued at all costs (even to the extent of preventing someone else taking a share in it) necessarily virtuous? Perhaps the stigma of 'not working' will be removed and five-day working (not to mention overtime) be made socially unacceptable? In short, maybe we exhalt work too much and allocate less time than we should to enjoying life with others. Handy (1984) is optimistic that we are moving, slowly but surely, towards new work patterns, and cites the growth of part-time work, DIY, non-work obligations and the informal economy as manifestations of this. He believes we are evolving from a materialist, employment-based society to a 'self-service society', in which work is being redefined, not by legislation, but by people creating new forms of work for themselves.

If such a move were to occur, and we switched our efforts and resources away from the goal of creating jobs for all to helping people manage without full-time employment, what implications would this have for the way our society is structured? In the first instance, it could mean that work is no longer done predominantly in a factory, office or shop, but in small workshops or from home. The idea that work has to be done five days a week, and between set times, becomes obsolete, and shift work and flexitime are already moves in this direction. There may also be shifts away from formal employment as fewer remain tied to particular firms and more work on contract. People could retire earlier, and the working week be cut (as advocated by the TUC) to allow available work to be spread more evenly. Jenkins and Sherman advocate a 'shorter working lifetime' to create larger blocks of time for people to travel, undertake sabbaticals, family activities etc. They envisage a situation in which by 2000 the working week could consist of three 8-hour days.

Job sharing
Much of this sounds attractive, but pessimists would argue that within the confines of capitalism and its prevailing ideologies there is no apparent mechanism for bringing such a transition about. The working wage is still the primary means by which wealth is distributed to the mass population, and work still principally means employment.

It is hard to see how we move away from this. How do we get the 80 per cent in employment to give up part of their work (and presumably their wage) on the promise that society could thereby be made more fulfilling, exciting and peaceful? We noted in Chapter 3 the dangers of a society polarized between those in full-time, highly-skilled, highly-paid occupations and an unemployed pool of up to 7 million, but is this not the direction in which we appear to be inexorably heading? The danger is that we could move into a society in which industrial collapse becomes so extensive that our entire social fabric breaks down. A small technocratic elite could control all forms of information, and a vast backwater economy emerge in which unemployment, menial work, crafts, moonlighting, barter and brigandry become standard features of everyday life. How do we avoid this and spread the available work more equitably to provide each worker with a 'smaller job'?

One obvious policy is some form of 'job sharing' which was proposed in 1982 by the then Employment Secretary Norman Tebbitt when he suggested voluntary 'job splitting' whereby grants would be given to companies who split jobs and kept people off the dole. He felt this could have particular appeal to the elderly and married women, but it was rejected by the TUC as 'an attempt to disguise the unemployment figures'. Trade unions are naturally cautious about job-sharing schemes as it could lead to a dilution of their control over a larger, dispersed, part-time workforce. Workers too are reluctant to embrace any scheme that might mean a drop in terms of pay, security or responsibility. Not that it should be thought, however, that trade unions are opposed to shorter working hours. On the contrary, they see this as the direction in which things must go, but the call is for a shorter working week and longer holidays (with no drop in pay) rather than job sharing. We still have the longest working week — around 40 hours on average — in Europe and the highest levels of overtime. Moreover, such demands are not confined to Britain. In West Germany, unions have pressed for a 35-hour working week, and in Japan — where the average worker puts in 2152 hours a year compared with 1910 in Britain, 1908 in the United States and 1656 in West Germany — the unions are making similar demands.

In many ways, job sharing and shorter working weeks sound much the same thing, but just as unions are suspicious of job sharing, so employers (especially in Britain) are cool on a shorter working week. In 1984, when the EEC tried to introduce shorter working hours to alleviate unemployment, Britain alone among the ten member states rejected the idea. The government argued that although it was not opposed 'in principle' to shorter hours, competitiveness remained the top priority, and Britain was in no position to reduce working hours if they remained high in Japan and the United States. We therefore reach a position where government, CBI and TUC all support shorter working hours in principle, yet offer not the slightest indication of any mutually agreed mechanism by which this might be achieved. Such changes only seem feasible in an atmosphere of mutual trust, understanding and compromise, and this seems noticeably absent.

A social wage

Even if agreement could be reached on shorter working hours, an even greater problem arises over the question of pay. Work is presently considered as *paid* employment, and the implication of people working in smaller jobs for shorter periods is that the form of remuneration will change. Keith Roberts (1982) proposes a national dividend paid to everyone, on top of which people could still earn as much as they like from employment. He assumes that people will need to do less work to achieve their desired standard of living, but this is problematic (for today's luxuries can become tomorrow's necessities) and will only occur if there is a marked change in existing work attitudes. Barry Jones similarly advocates a society in which income should be a right to economic support, not a reward for work, and in which the right to work (and not to work) is guaranteed for all.

These, and similar proposals, are far more feasible in theory than practice, but they do seem the direction in which we have to go if we are to avoid the social polarization and upheaval mentioned earlier. The implication is that eventually, instead of being rewarded for output and effort, workers will be paid according to need, and issued with a 'social wage' as of a right of citizenship. This may smack of Marx ('from each according to his ability, to each according to his needs') but, given that the unemployed are already paid a social wage (unemployment benefit), why should this not be extended to the rest of the population? The emphasis would now be on consumption rather than production; the stigma of not working would be removed; overtime would be outlawed; and greater encouragement given to work-related leisure activities.

Various suggestions have been made as to how, in the short term, we could ease such a transition by adopting certain legislative measures. In the first place, one could offer tax concessions to people prepared to give up some work to others, or the fifth day of work could be more heavily taxed (as in the case of overtime). Employers are presently penalized for employing more people, and this could be eased if firms paid far lower national insurance contributions for short-time workers (and an increased rate for full-time workers). Similarly, employers might even be subsidized for employing *more* workers in short-time jobs. A further measure would be to legally limit the amount of overtime worked: in West Germany, the legal limit is 60 hours and in Belgium 65, but similar restrictions do not operate in Britain. Evidence suggests that the role of the state is vital in initiating and supporting change, and those countries with established tripartite machinery seem at the moment best able to introduce new schemes for working hours, wages and work conditions.

The problem is that our economy is designed to fit the conventional patterns of big business and big government, and work is regarded as embracing employment by large-scale organizations. People are seen as relying either on an employer for a wage or the state for the dole, and it is difficult for government to break free from this pattern. We have a deep-rooted system of rigidity, embodied in tax, company and employment legislation, which makes change extremely difficult. The whole capitalist system (including various financial allocations from government) encourages capital investment, which inevitably means further automation. The focus is on technological innovation rather than employment creation (though capitalism's defenders would claim that the former assists the latter), and large organizations are not well placed to change their attitudes or develop the small-scale, decentralized, informal, local work patterns that many now advocate. As James Robertson (1983) has noted, in the early nineteenth century the Whigs and Tories refused to accept that Britain was ceasing to be an agricultural country and, by delaying the repeal of the Corn Laws, put off the introduction of cheap food and caused much unnecessary hardship and distress. We could now be going through an equally profound transition, and politicians may again be similarly unable, or unwilling, to respond to the situation.

THE POLITICAL RESPONSE

Since 1985 the three major political groupings — and particularly certain individuals such as Neil Kinnock, Shirley Williams and Francis Pym — have taken up the 'work issue', but most of this discussion is still couched in traditional terms. Various reports refer to 'new work patterns' but contain little indication as to *how* we bring them about. All three party groups still seem to share the basic ideology of unlimited growth, and see technology as a tool for enhancing efficiency and providing the greater material wealth we all desire. Of course, politicians are psychologically tuned to the short term — the next election — and most of their concern is with the here-and-now rather than the long-term future, but such an approach skirts the issues raised in this chapter. There appears to be no widespread discussion of how we adopt new work patterns; no debates on truly radical policies such as a social wage; and no apparent awareness of the societal dangers that may unfurl. Concern over these questions raises the debate to a higher level and poses questions over the uses of technology. Should we automatically adopt technology just because it happens to be available, cheaper, faster, more reliable or whatever? Perhaps we should question technology's role; ponder its ceaseless development; and ask whether its application is always the 'force for good' that some would have us believe. In short, perhaps we should more closely examine the options before us.

One political party that is addressing these issues is the Green (formerly the Ecology) Party which put up 108 candidates in the 1983 election. The heart of the ecology argument is that technological development and economic growth have become gods in our society but that there are environmental limits (e.g. energy) to continued economic expansion. They claim we already have enough to meet people's basic needs and should escape from the treadmill of ever greater production and consumption: the economics of more and more should be replaced with the economics of enough. On new technology, the Ecology Party's 1983 manifesto said: 'As the new microchip technology begins to bite, unemployment is going to get dramatically worse, which is why we must find some new way of dividing up the national cake that does not necessarily depend on people having a job.' This was the only manifesto to accept as inevitable an increase in unemployment, and advocated a national income scheme under which everyone (whether in work or not) should get a basic income payment to replace social security benefits and tax allowances, which could lead to a reduction in hours worked, overtime, large-scale working, full-time working etc. We would pay less attention to the quantity of work undertaken and more to the *quality* of work: this should be judged not by its profitability or productivity, but by its usefulness and intrinsic satisfaction to the worker. *New* jobs could be created in such areas as energy conservation, development of alternative energy resources, combined heat and power schemes, small-scale mixed farming, labour-intensive food production, land reclamation, recycling and reuse, housing renovation, rural regeneration, repair and maintenance etc.

APPROPRIATE TECHNOLOGY

Despite the fairly recent emergence of the Ecology/Green Party, this viewpoint in fact has a longer tradition in the writings of Ellul (1965), Mumford (1967), Illich (1973), Schumacher (1974), Dickson (1974) and Robertson (1983). Ellul argues that technology is basically antagonistic to human values and the danger is that it comes to dominate man. We become obsessed with technique — which emphasizes means rather than ends — and discussion over *how* something should be done obliterates debate as to whether it *ought* to be done. Because technique dictates, man loses the freedom to choose.

This school are not 'anti-technology' but believe we must use it to provide tools rather than machines, and should carefully consider the way it is applied. The proposal is that technologies, including new information technology, should be used to create a society with devolved structures, limited growth and low energy; in short, they should be used in an 'appropriate' manner. Mumford believes we are obsessed with (a) faster, (b) farther away, (c) bigger and (d) more; the effect of which is to remove limits, hasten the pace of change, smooth out seasonal and regional differences, standardize internationally etc. This brings us back to the concerns raised in the Introduction. Whereas the 1960s may have been a period of technological optimism (with man reaching the moon), considerable doubts are now raised as to technology's ability to solve human problems such as famine, poverty and international conflict. The danger is that we develop a fatalist conviction that a technological solution exists for everything, and the more complex a situation is, the less likely debate is to occur. We come to accept that we have no choice but to build nuclear power stations and motorways, and a false dichotomy is forced on us whereby technology equals rationality and progress while resistance is irrational and reactionary. Must we always accept the *highest* technology available, or are there varieties of technologies and choices to be made? Because something is technologically possible (or profitable), does this mean it must be pursued? Are electric carving knives 'rational' when humans are starving in third world countries? Are sophisticated nuclear weapons 'progress'? Even if we choose a particular technology, there are still further decisions as to how it should be applied. Some cities built freeways to encourage the use of private cars (e.g. Los Angeles) while others concentrated on effective public transport systems (e.g. Stockholm). All these arguments apply to the chip. Technological determinism suggests that technology is a single entity and that its effects are universal; but outcomes are much more a matter of political choice.

Probably the best-known exponent on these lines is E. F. Schumacher (1974) who, in *Small is Beautiful, Biggest is Best*, argues for reversing economies of scale. Instead of *more* things being produced by fewer people using high technology, we might inflict less damage and violence on society and the environment if more people produced *enough* things with low technology. He argues that small-scale labour-intensive industries serving regional needs should be encouraged instead of being squeezed out by the large capital-intensive firms.

Schumacher's work raises five major concerns:

- Modern production is based on the use of fossil fuels which are 'natural capital' and cannot be replaced. Industrial society therefore consumes the very bases on which it is erected, and treats irreplaceable capital (e.g. oil) as income.
- Pollution is a major problem as little thought is given to the recycling of products. There are 'tolerance margins of nature', and city smog, river pollution etc. show little sign of abatement. Some of the most advanced industrialized societies have the greatest public squalor and pollution. Why should we assume that further growth will rectify this situation?
- There is a danger of increased specialization and centralization. Small enterprises provide more personal control, more rewarding jobs etc., and are better placed to provide socially useful goods at suitable prices.
- Technology has proved ineffective in solving many of the third world's problems. The 'green revolution' did not end food shortages; new high-yield crops have been found to have low resistance to disease; fertilizers and other aids have proved expensive; and generally the quality of food has, if anything, been reduced.
- Technological advance can endanger the planet. Vast amounts are still spent on defence, supersonic aircraft, nuclear power stations etc., and the risks from this are high.

Schumacher advocates the use of natural foods to retain soil fertility; urges the use of small-scale technology so that workers can feel part of an organization; and calls for less emphasis on economic growth and production. To repeat, he is not anti-technology, but is concerned as to its application, organization and control. The *appropriate* use of new information technology could prove highly beneficial to mankind, but the danger is that moral and social aspects become secondary to economic considerations. He questions the convergence writers' argument that third world countries should necessarily industrialize on the lines of the West. He also suggests that public ownership may be necessary to achieve social rather than economic goals, but private ownership is accept-able if small-scale. The key factor is size rather than ownership, though the two are inevitably inter-related.

Various labels have been used to describe socially useful technologies. Dickson talks of alternative technology, Illich of con-vivial technology, while terms such as people's technology or soft technology are also used. The theme is essentially the same — that continuous exponential growth is neither inevitable nor desirable and technology should reflect the genuine needs of society. Some emphasize ecological issues such as pollution (e.g. Clarke) and others political issues like control (e.g. Dickson), but basically appropriate technology means that it should be intelligible to, and controlled by, the local community; use indigenous resources and skills to provide socially useful products; offer safe, purposeful employment; and be non-pollutant, ecologically sound and (wherever possible) capable of re-cyclement.

ALTERNATIVE SCENARIOS

A continuing theme of this book has been that we cannot state precisely what will happen, but as regards work patterns we can now at least summarize a number of alternative scenarios. The first is the optimistic view that nothing much will change or that, if it does, it will only get better. More work, and more interesting work, can be provided in an increasingly affluent, democratic, open, meritocratic — in short, superior — society. Work has traditionally meant jobs, and there is every reason to think that more of these can be created following the introduction of new technology. This view still finds favour (for different reasons) at both ends of the British political spectrum, for the Conservative government believe jobs can be created through market forces while many in the opposition maintain this can be achieved through the state. Personally, I believe both views underestimate the degree of change we can expect and offer traditional remedies for novel situations. Neither wing talks in terms of alternative scenarios, but rather the restoration of full employment.

This gains little support from those pessimists who maintain that unemployment — high enough already — will only get worse as a result of new technology. They fear that we could simply come to accept unemployment as an inevitable part of modern life, and rationalize its existence as the necessary price for keeping inflation under control and making our society industrially competitive. Unemployment is seen as preferable to international poverty and if it means some going without work this is unfortunate, but unavoidable.

Our society has already gone a long way towards accepting this view. Unemployment of nearly 4 million is tolerated and, as Handy points out, we often explain away the situation by convincing ourselves that the unemployed either don't want work (i.e. the scroungers); don't need work (e.g. married women); or don't deserve work (e.g. the unskilled). This may clear the consciences of the employed but, as a long-term recipe for social stability, it seems disastrous. The economic cost will run to many billions and the social cost will be the polarization discussed in Chapter 3.

A third alternative is a 'leisure scenario' in which technology provides all our basic wants and allows us to pursue a life of true leisure. As we have seen, this can be viewed optimistically or pessimistically: people may either pursue considerably enriched leisure-time activities or, alternatively, lead lives of mindless boredom broken only by the endless trivia pumped out by media barons. The key point is that when optimists talk of 'enriched leisure', what they really mean is that leisure takes on work connotations. A society based on idleness — such as the unemployed experience now — is not a serious consideration, for people must be given the opportunity to develop interests and skills. When we talk of the 'leisure classes' of the past, we should recall that they worked hard — at governing, running their estates, patronizing the arts etc. — and never pursued a life-style of total leisure.

This brings us to an 'activity scenario', and the one I would broadly advocate. Our need is to re-think work; to extend it beyond merely 'doing a job' to embrace non-work obligations, home crafts, DIY etc. We must escape from the treadmill whereby work means employment, and employment means a wage. Work and leisure should increasingly merge into each other to form activity. Such a transition will not be easy, for as we have seen it contains important implications for employment legislation, welfare benefits, income distribution etc., but it increasingly appears the most sensible way forward. It requires us to appreciate the nature of the debates and to raise our sights to broader issues concerning the whole nature of our society. Most important of all, it requires us to examine our own assumptions and prejudices, for we are blinkered by an industrial culture which makes it difficult for us to consider appropriate choices.

CHAPTER TEN

People and Chips

Many have written of 'people and chips' and how one affects the other. I have suggested that this society/technology interface, and particularly as it relates to new information technology, can be usefully explored through two main perspectives which I have labelled optimists and pessimists. The first group start with the technology; highlight the various benefits it can offer; and incline to the view that a predominant form of technology pervades a given epoch. Technology is the independent variable and, in the case of the microchip, it enables us to experience a new industrial revolution and reap the fruits of post-industrial society. Pessimists, on the other hand, who comprise a more diverse group and can be considered at different levels, tend to see technology as the dependent variable — a social product — and more the result of dominant economic and political forces. The optimistic view generally finds favour on the political right, and the pessimistic on the political left.

These two approaches (summarized in Table 2.1) adopt different stances towards society, technology, the social structure, the nature of work etc., and I attempted to show how they can be applied to a discussion of the human effects of new information technology. In each chapter, I argued that the particular concerns of the two camps varied according to context, and indicated this by adopting further labels, as summarized in Fig. 10.1.

I used Bell and Braverman as representative of the different ends of this continuum and, in applying the model to particular issues, branded various writers as either optimists (e.g. Evans, Toffler, Minford, Leontief, Blauner, Guiliano, Tapper etc.) or pessimists

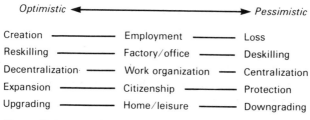

Figure 10.1   Main concerns of the contrasting perspectives

(e.g. Reinecke, Dickson, Jenkins and Sherman, Cooley, Downing, Hewitt, Hood etc.).

A final word though on labels and, in particular, optimists and pessimists. I stressed at the outset that they must be used with care and always in context, for the pessimists in particular can be considered at different levels, which allows certain writers to be pessimistic in one sense, but optimistic in another.

A particular danger is that the labels carry with them certain connotations. The optimist is seen as forward-looking, hopeful and positive, while the pessimist is presented as miserable, downcast and a die-hard conservative reluctant to change. Technology itself is invariably presented as 'progressive', which provides the optimists with a far better public image, for to oppose it is seen as irrational, reactionary and Luddite. This often allows conservatives, as in the case of employment, to portray themselves as radicals, boldly marching forward into the micro-based, post-industrial society. In short, they present a positive approach to technology through the continuation of existing policies and attitudes: the adoption of conservative means to meet radical ends. Many pessimists on the political left, however, branded by their opponents as timid, unrealistic, obstructive and dogmatic, would reject the accusation of being reactionary and indeed apply it to their critics. They share the vision of a 'better' society and are pessimistic, not towards technology which they concede can provide substantial human benefits, but over its likely use in capitalist society, or particular government policies. No doubt they would prefer to be labelled realists.

The danger over labels can be illustrated in the work of Jenkins and Sherman. In Chapter 3, I termed them pessimists over the employment issue because they foresaw a 'collapse of work' whether we adopt new technology or not; but overall, theirs is not a pessimistic book. As they say

> It is a prospect at which we should not quail or rush to the nearest bunker. This is an opportunity to rethink our traditional attitudes and to accept boldly the new opportunities. It is an occasion for hope, not despair.

This is an optimistic outlook, accompanied by a radical programme for social transformation which would utilize the higher prosperity and greater leisure time now available to the working population. Conversely, Reay Atkinson (1980), while 'moderately optimistic' that new information technology will not lead to considerable labour displacement, doubts whether Britain is prepared for or able to grasp the new opportunities. Whether particular writers are optimistic or pessimistic about a particular issue is therefore not necessarily a reflection of how they see the effects of new technology as a whole, or even on another issue. This is why I cautioned over the use of labels at the outset and have often used them in quotation marks to reflect differences in interpretation.

Despite these dangers, however, I feel that the two approaches provide a useful framework for collating and considering the wide range of discussion now emerging on the human implications of new information technology. I am aware that there are many important areas I have not covered: the effects of further technological advances such as biotechnology and artificial intelligence; likely applications in motoring, medicine, education, welfare services etc.; social issues such as crime; occupational changes in banking, insurance, printing, hospitals, police etc.; and, most important of all, global issues such as nuclear weaponry and the third world. The arguments, however, would remain much the same. As we noted in the Introduction, some regard sophisticated weaponry as the safeguard of civilization (optimists), while others see it as the major threat to life on our planet (pessimists). Similarly with the third world, some claim new information technology will stimulate the less developed economies while others see it intensifying the existing control of advanced nations. Convergence writers may see new technology as the key to the door of industrialization (and then post-industrialization) for third world countries, while pessimists foresee a growing polarization between rich and poor as the multi-nationals control any technological development on their terms (e.g. allowing chip manufacture to be done in less advanced countries by cheap, unskilled labour, while research and development is retained within the advanced economies).

A new industrial revolution? Not necessarily. The chip may be revolutionary in a technological sense — and book titles such as *Micro revolution* and *Microelectronics revolution* perfectly justified — but this is not the same as saying that such developments represent a revolution in the broader social, political and economic sense. The new technologies *could* result in a new industrial revolution, but at the moment such predictions seem premature.

I therefore reject an optimistic view which suggests that technological advancement will automatically transform and improve all aspects of social life. This is probably most glowingly presented by Masuda when he writes:

> We are moving towards the twenty-first century with the very great goal of building a Computopia on earth, the historical monument of which will be only several chips one inch square in a small box. But that box will store many historical records, including the record of how 4 billion world citizens overcame the energy crisis and the population explosion, achieved the abolition of nuclear weapons and complete disarmament, conquered illiteracy, and created a rich symbiosis of god and man, without the compulsion of power or law, but by the voluntary cooperation of the citizens to put into practice their common global aims.

This seems to me 'optimism gone mad' and I see little justification for such a scenario; certainly not in the forseeable future. But just as I cannot accept that technology will impose a certain form of society, so equally I reject the highly pessimistic view which suggests that technology is wholly implemented and controlled by those holding economic and political power, and I do so on the same grounds: that it is over-deterministic and ignores the importance of choice. Both polar views suggest, for different reasons, that we are powerless in the face of technological change, and that as individuals and groups we have no say over its introduction. Any technology certainly contains societal implications, and those holding power unquestionably influence its application, but the recurring theme of this book has been that within these parameters, individuals — through political parties, trade unions, community groups etc. — can significantly affect the way it is used. It is like travelling by car on a motorway: we cannot turn back, and the technology of the vehicle imposes certain constraints on us. Similarly, the route and regulations are determined by those with the power to build and control motorways. But within these limits we can exercise choices — over the turns we take, the speed we travel or the extent to which we consider others — and can make demands for changes in speed limits, car design, safety provisions etc.

Various key words have appeared throughout this book — convergence, innovation, revolution, deskilling etc. — but probably the most important is choice. We should be careful over global predictions, for the outcome is influenced by how and where technology is used. It is not possible to formulate conclusions in simple cause and effect terms. The wide range of applications can lead to a similarly wide range of effects, many of which may be in very different directions. So much depends on the *particular* — the particular society, legislative framework, government policies, workplace, management style, household, even individual — and the choices that are made. In each chapter, as we explored different facets, we discovered wide variations in application, and the deeper we investigated, the more the level of analysis seemed to be pushed down — down to the bottom point of our 'up-turned conceptual triangle' (Fig. 2.2), and the issue of choice. There *are* choices to be made: between removing skills and enhancing them; between hierarchical and democratic systems; between technical and human factors etc. I have included a wide range of opinions as to what various commentators think *likely* to happen; but what *will* happen depends on the outcome of a multitude of various decision-making processes.

In saying this, I do not suggest global discussions are without value, for they raise important questions and help us focus the debate. The contribution of the optimists is to show us the benefits that new information technology has the potential to provide. The contribution of the pessimists is to point out that these are by no means certain; to make us aware of threats and dangers; and to help us make informed choices.

In periods of change, there are greater opportunities for making individual choices and yet, paradoxically, at such times we often feel incapable of doing so. New technology deepens and widens all our choices and makes us hesitant: we are better informed than ever before, but the stakes are higher. We can use technology to expand our freedoms in democratic, pluralist society or allow moves towards far greater tyrannical, dictatorial control. We can cure disease and feed the hungry, or pollute the atmosphere and blow ourselves to pieces. This is described by Cooley as a choice between 'architect or bee': human beings can either be reduced to bee-like behaviour in which they react to the technology specified for them, or they can be architects designing the use of technology to enhance human creativity and individual freedoms. These are stark alternatives, and they ultimately depend on political decisions.

I stated at the outset that my aim was not to preach a particular line but rather to consider and contrast the various lines being preached. My intention has not been to provide answers but to pose questions, supply information, increase awareness, raise issues, and offer a framework within which the reader can better appreciate the various debates. We cannot specify what will happen, for the overriding theme is uncertainty. I am not concerned with predicting the future, but rather with the *options* that face individuals, organizations, communities and societies. My own view is therefore merely one more, and far less important than that the reader should develop his or her own views on the subject, but I sense that my personal prejudices have surfaced from time to time and that to omit them altogether might seem cowardly.

In rejecting the polar positions, laying particular emphasis on choice, and advocating a contingency approach, I find myself on most issues occupying the centre ground of the continuum. I say this, not for convenience, but from conviction. I am sure there is much to feel positive about with regard to new information technology, particularly in the home, in medicine and travel, in connection with certain mundane and dangerous jobs, and with regard to greater opportunities for leisure. But I am bound to say that I share many of the pessimists' misgivings. I am concerned over threats to employment and individual freedoms; further deskilling in much factory and office work; the trivialization of broadcasting; and our ability to make the necessary transition to an 'activity-based' society. Particularly in Britain, with current policies, I see little indication that the microchip is providing the boost to democracy — either at work or in general — that many optimists predict, and I am equally concerned over ecological issues and the dangers from nuclear holocaust. Hopefully by increasing awareness and encouraging the exercise of choice, as this book attempts to do, we stand a better chance of avoiding these pitfalls. My own position can be summed up simply: I look forward to what new technology might do *for* me; I dread what it might do *to* me.

Bibliography and Further Reading

Advisory Council for Applied Research and Development (ACARD) (1980) *Technological Change: threats and opportunities for the United Kingdom*, London, HMSO.

Arthur Andersen and Co. (1985) *Trends in Information Technology*, Chicago, Arthur Andersen.

Atkinson, R. (1980) 'The employment consequences of computers; a user view', in Forester, T. (ed.) (1980).

Bell, D. (1974) *The Coming of Post-Industrial Society*, London, Heinemann.

Bell, D. (1979) 'The Social Framework of the Information Society', in Dertouzos, M. L. and Moses, J. (eds) *The Computer Age: a twenty-year view*, Cambridge, Mass., The MIT Press. Also in Forester, T. (ed.) (1980).

Benson, I. and Lloyd, J. (1983) *New Technology and Industrial Change*, London, Kogan Page.

Blau, P. M. and Schoenherr, R. A. (1973) 'New forms of power', in Salaman, G. and Thompson, K. (eds) *People and Organizations*, London, Longmans.

Blauner, R. (1964) *Alienation and Freedom*, Chicago, University of Chicago Press.

Braverman, H. (1974) *Labour and Monopoly Capital*, New York, Monthly Review Press.

Burns, A. (1981) *The Microchip: appropriate or inappropriate technology?*, Chichester, Ellis Horwood.

Child, J. (1984) *Organization: a guide to problems and practice*, London, Harper and Row.

Clarke, R. (1982) *Work in crisis: the dilemma of a nation*, St Andrew's, St Andrew's Press.

Cohen, R. (1984) *Whose file is it anyway?*, London, National Council for Civil Liberties.

Confederation of British Industry (CBI) (1980) *Jobs — facing the future; a CBI discussion document*, London, CBI.

Conference of Socialist Economists (1980) *Microelectronics: capitalist technology and the working class*, London, CSE Books.

Cooley, M. (1980) *Architect or Bee? The human/technology relationship*, Slough, Langley Technical Services.

Cooley, M. (1984) 'Computers, Politics and Unemployment', in Sieghart, P. (ed.) (1984).

Cooper, C. L. and Cox, A. (1985) 'Occupational Stress among word processor operators', *Stress Medicine*, Vol. 1, No. 2, April/June.

Crozier, M. (1983) 'Implications for the Organization', in Otway, H. J. and Peltu, M. (eds) *New Office Technology: human and organizational aspects*, London, Francis Pinter.

Dawson, J. (1984) 'A medical case history', in Sieghart, P. (ed.) (1984).

Deane, P. (1965) *The First Industrial Revolution*, Cambridge, Cambridge University Press.

Dickson, D. (1974) *Alternative technology and the politics of technical change*, London, Fontana.

Downing, H. (1980) 'Word processors and the oppression of women', in Forester, T. (ed.) (1980).

Ellul, J. (1965) *The Technological Society*, London, Cape.

Evans, C. (1979) *The Mighty Micro*, London, Victor Gollancz.

Forester, T. (1978) 'The Microelectronic Revolution', *New Society*, 9 November.

Forester, T. (ed.) (1980) *The Microelectronics Revolution*, Oxford, Basil Blackwell.

Forester, T. (ed.) (1985) *The Information Technology Revolution*, Oxford, Basil Blackwell.

Guiliano, V. E. (1982) 'The Mechanization of Office Work', *Scientific American*, September. Also in Forester, T. (ed.) (1985).

Handy, C. (1984) *The Future of Work*, Oxford, Basil Blackwell.

Hewitt, P. (1984) 'What's in a file?', in Sieghart, P. (ed.) (1984).

Hood, S. (1984) 'The politics of information power', in Sieghart, P. (ed.) (1984).

Huws, U. (1982) 'The chip on whose shoulder? The effects of new technology upon female employment', *The Guardian*, 5 November.

Illich, I. (1973) *Tools for conviviality*, London, Fontana.

Jenkins, C. and Sherman, B. (1979) *The Collapse of Work*, London, Eyre Methuen.

Jenkins, C. and Sherman, B. (1981) *The Leisure Shock*, London, Eyre Methuen.

Jones, B. (1982) *Sleepers Wake*, Brighton, Wheatsheaf Books Ltd.

Jones, F. (1981) 'The Word Processor — a case study in introducing a microelectronic system', in Twiss, B. C. (ed.) *The Managerial Implications of Microelectronics*, London, Macmillan.

Jones, T. (ed.) (1980) *Microelectronics and Society*, Milton Keynes, The Open University Press.

Kerr, C., Dunlop, J. T., Harbison, F. and Myers, C. A. (1973) *Industrialism and Industrial Man*, Harmondsworth, Penguin.

Kerr, C. (1983) *The Future of Industrial Societies*, Cambridge, Mass., Harvard University Press.

Kondratiev, N. (1925) 'The Long Waves of Economic Life', in *Readings in Business Cycle Theory*, American Economic Association, 1950.

Labour Party Microelectronics Working Group (1980) *Microelectronics*, London, The Labour Party.

Large, P. (1984) *The Micro Revolution Revisited*, London, Francis Pinter.

Leontief, W. (1985) *The Impact of Automation on Employment 1963–2000*, Oxford, Oxford University Press.

Martin, J. (1978) *The Wired Society*, Englewood Cliffs, N.J., Prentice Hall.

Masuda, Y. (1981) *The Information Society, as post-industrial society*, Tokyo, Institute for the Information Society.

Minford, P. (1984) 'High unemployment is not permanent', *Economic Affairs*, Vol. 4, No. 4, July–September.

Mumford, L. (1967) *The Myth of the Machine*, London, Secker and Warburg.

National Economic Development Council (NEDC) (1982) *Technology: the issues for the distributive trades*, London, NEDC.

National Economic Development Council (NEDC) (1982) *Policy for the UK Electronics Industry*, London, NEDC.

Parker, S. (1983) *Leisure and Work*, London, Allen and Unwin.

Piercy, N. (ed.) (1984) *The Management Implications of New Information Technology*, Beckenham, Croom Helm.

Reinecke, I. (1984) *Electronic Illusions*, Harmondsworth, Penguin.

Roberts, K. (1982) *Automation, Unemployment, and the Redistribution of Income*, European Centre for Work and Society.

Robertson, J. (1983) *The Sane Alternative*, Ironbridge, James Robertson.

Rosenbrock, H. *et al.* (1981) *New Technology: society, employment and skill*, London, the Council for Science and Society. Also in Forester, T. (ed.) (1985).

Rowan, T. (1982) *Managing with Computers*, London, Heinemann.

Rowe, C. (1984) 'The break-up of computer services departments: the effects of the micro', *Industrial Management and Data Systems*, MCB University Press, January/February.

Rowe, C. (1984) 'How will the new technology affect the office secretary?', *The British Journal of Administrative Management*, The Institute of Administrative Management, Vol. 34, No. 6, October.

Rowe, C. (1984) 'The impact of computers on the work organization', *Industrial Management and Data Systems*, MCB University Press, November/December.

Schumacher, E. F. (1974) *Small is beautiful; a study of economics as if people mattered*, London, Abacus.

Sieghart, P. (ed.) (1984) *Microchips with everything; the consequences of information technology*, London, Comedia Publishing Group.

Simons, G. (1985) *Silicon Shock; the menace of the computer invasion*, Oxford, Basil Blackwell.

Sleigh, J., Boatwright, B., Irwin, P. and Stangon, R. (1979) *The manpower implications of microelectronic technology*, the Department of Employment Manpower Study Group, London, HMSO.

Stonier, T. (1979) *The third industrial revolution, microprocessors and robots*, IMF Central Committee Meeting, Vienna.

Stonier, T. (1982) *The Wealth of Information: a profile of the post-industrial society*, London, Methuen.

Stonier, T. (1984) 'Learning a hard lesson about living with hitech', *The Guardian*, 28 March.

Tapper, C. (1983) *Computer Law*, London, Longmans.

Taylor, F. W. (1911) *The Principles of Scientific Management*, New York, Harper and Row.

Toffler, A. (1980) *The Third Wave*, London, Collins.

Warr, P. and Wall, T. (1975) *Work and Well-being*, Harmondsworth, Penguin.

Watson, T. (1980) *Sociology, Work and Industry*, London, Routledge and Kegan Paul.

Williams, V. (1984) 'Employment implications of new technology', *Employment Gazette*, May.

Zorkoczy, P. (1985) *Information Technology; an introduction*, London, Pitman.

Index